To journalists around the world who dare to seek and tell the truth, no matter what the consequences—and to those who lost their lives in doing so.

Also By Chip Scanlan

Writers on Writing: Inside the Lives of 55 Distinguished Writers and Editors

Writers on Writing: The Journal

News Writing and Reporting: The Complete Guide for Today's Journalist

The Holly Wreath Man

America's Best Newspaper Writing

Reporting and Writing: Basics for the 21st Century

More 33 Ways!

33 Ways Not to Screw up Your Business Emails

33 Ways Not to Screw Up Creative Entrepreneurship

33 Ways Not to Screw Up Consulting

33 Ways Not to Screw Up Your Financial Life

Find out more about the series at www.33WaysSeries.com

"Journalism is what we need to make democracy work."

Walter Cronkite

Contents

Introduction

Journalism is in trouble. But it's not too late to save it—or yourselves—by mastering, sharing and implementing the most critical skills any reporter can have: the basics.

Journalists are often thrown into their craft, with the most rudimentary understanding of what it means to be a journalist in a democracy.

Consider this book a survival manual.

Journalism uniquely has the power to hold up a mirror and show us all who we really are, regardless of ideology, identity or place.

It is a discipline that, at its best, breaks through walls of deceit to shine a light on solutions to our world's most complicated problems. Using timeless storytelling techniques, journalists illuminate the human condition.

Anne Janzer says in her book "Writing to Be Understood, "We need people who communicate across chasms in beliefs and understanding, healing the divisiveness that characterizes current public debate." That's the job of the journalist.

Whether you are a student, a recent college grad or have decades of experience in a newsroom, this book teaches, or reacquaints you with, new and tried-and-tested ways to design, protect, and grow the journalism we all need.

BRACING FOR NEW CHALLENGES

Right now, the news industry is in free fall. Over the last 15 years, a toxic blend of economic, technological and social forces has eliminated nearly 1,800 newspapers, millions of readers, and tens of thousands of jobs.

News deserts—communities without any local newspapers—dot America's landscape. National papers thrive, yet local news markets don't always share their economic success. Coverage of school board meetings, crime, government actions, and school sports that knit a community together disappears when a newspaper dies and journalists aren't there to make their essential contribution to society: to bear witness. Labor-intensive investigative reporting that holds the powerful accountable usually disappears too. Diversity in hiring and promotion, a vital component of inclusivity in news coverage, continues to lag.

Meanwhile, hedge funds cannibalize ailing newspapers for profit, slash staffs and sell off vacant newspaper offices.

But there is hope.

Journalists and philanthropists are joining forces to create digital news startups around the country. Multimedia and data reporting have created exciting opportunities for newcomers.

Whatever the distribution method, humanity's abiding need to know what's new will always support a market for competent journalists.

HOW TO USE THIS BOOK

In two decades as a journalist, I made many of the mistakes described in these pages. Good editors and generous colleagues showed me how to stop repeating them. Working as a writing teacher and coach in the 30 years since I left the newsroom has taught me new lessons about my profession.

This book brings together 33 examples of ways to screw up your journalism and the best practices that can correct them. It draws on research, personal experience, and interviews with reporters, editors, publishers and journalism professors who gave their time and insights to help you excel. Some of the material here appeared, in different form, in my Poynter Institute blog, Chip on Your Shoulder; my current newsletter, Chip's Writing Lessons, and my two college-level textbooks.

My advice is to read the book through once, making note of which chapters speak to you at that moment. Then dip in for inspiration and instruction or consult a relevant chapter when you face a particularly thorny problem—at your desk or before you head out into the field.

According to a 2021 Gallup poll, only about one-third of Americans trust the mass media to report the news fully, accurately and fairly, the second-lowest portion on record.

The topics covered in this book's chapters will help you regain that trust by dodging the potholes and land mines that cause journalists and their audiences misery.

Whatever your role in a newsroom or level of experience, I hope you'll find something that can help or remind you of a lesson learned or that you can share with others. If you're a teacher, an editor or a coach, the same holds true.

Journalism is a vital profession that takes tenacity, courage and intelligence. But it also can be fun. Let's begin!

#1: Being Inhuman

Journalists don't care about people. They only care about getting their stories. When tragedy strikes, they descend like locusts. Network anchors show up like royalty. The mob barrels over each other to pester grief-stricken survivors. When the newsworthy stream of interest trickles out, they disappear as fast as they came.

Sadly, there's more than a little truth to that picture. It's a big reason why, polls show, the public views journalists with such disdain, compounded by the present polarized political and social climate. Scan reporters' Twitter and Facebook feeds and you'll see the vitriol, even rape and death threats.

NOT EVERY JOURNALIST IS HEARTLESS

The best reporters I know don't barge in when tragedy strikes. They leave notes at the door saying that they're there to listen if someone wants to talk.

"I am a human first," Carolyn Mungo, vice president and station manager at WFAA-TV in Dallas, told me. "People have to see that journalists are not just a body behind a microphone. Even if you have five minutes, don't rush, let them know you care."

The long-held stereotype of the journalist as a creep with a notepad is ingrained in the public mind, fueled in part by distorted portrayals in popular culture. A 2020 Pew Research Center poll found "the public is more likely than not to say that news organizations do not care about the people they report on."

I know too many caring and ethical reporters that contradict this finding, but it reflects a sobering reality that journalists need to keep in mind when they encounter people, especially at times of tragedy. On an individual level, they can push back against the public's view of the journalist.

1. Be respectful. Ask yourself how you would want to be treated if you were in a traumatic situation. Lynsey Addario, a Pulitzer Prize–winning photojournalist with The New York Times, took the iconic photograph of a Ukrainian woman, her two children and a volunteer killed by Russian shelling on March 6, 2022, as they tried to flee hostilities in the town of Irpin. She and her colleagues eventually contacted the husband, who had been away caring for his ailing mother. He agreed to talk with them. Yet, when he visited the morgue to see his dead family, they chose not to accompany him. "We decided it was too personal," Addario told Michael Barbaro, host of the Times' podcast, "The Daily." "We didn't want to bother him at that moment." He later gave them an interview for a heartbreaking story about the lives and final hours of the family he lost.

2. Respond to your emails and tweets from readers and viewers, even criticism (when it's sent in good faith). Ignore or block the insults or hate-mongers.

3. Empathize. If you can show subjects that you have some understanding of their situation, they're more likely to open up to you.

4. Ask your news organization to sponsor meet-and-greets with the public. People need to know about journalists like Helen Ubiñas, a Philadelphia Inquirer columnist who shows up at schools with reporter's notebooks, chocolates, and pens branded with the query "Tips? Story Ideas?" and her Twitter handle. She organizes annual anti-gun violence rallies that draw hundreds of young people.

BEING HUMAN PAYS OFF

Once, I was assigned a story about a young woman caught in the crossfire between police and a desperate criminal. She was killed shortly before her wedding day.

At the family's door, I wanted to flee.

Instead, I gulped and told her father, "I just didn't want you to pick up the paper and say, 'Couldn't they at least have asked if we wanted to say something?'" Within moments, I was in the young woman's bedroom, admiring the gifts that filled her hope chest, poignant details that made it into my story.

"Trauma is central to human existence," said Jan Winburn, who sent journalists to many tragic scenes during her career as a top CNN editor. "Sometimes that means illuminating the landscape of tragedy and trauma."

Take care of yourself. Covering trauma can cause intense stress and even burnout. Consider seeking therapy, with the support of your newsroom leaders, if you feel overwhelmed by reporting on traumatic events.

The Dart Center, at Columbia University's Graduate School of Journalism, offers training, handbooks and other resources for journalists covering trauma.

Being human on any story enables you to do your job better. It may also change people's attitudes about you and your fellow journalists.

#2: Bad Attitude

When I think of the hundreds of journalists I have worked with, interviewed or coached over the years, the best ones impressed me with their intellect and creativity. But what stands out most are not these strengths, important as they are. Instead, it was their attitude that made them special.

Five decades of working with writers and editors has convinced me that attitude—a way of thinking that is reflected in a person's behavior—matters more than talent.

Talent may open the door, but attitude gets you inside the room.

Journalism is a craft. It relies on a set of skills: generating story ideas, reporting and researching, writing and revision (and more revision), understanding of structure, and facility with language, syntax, and style. Mastery requires years of study, work and above all, patience.

In his book "Outliers: The Story of Success," Malcolm Gladwell cites research that found achieving mastery in many fields requires 10,000 hours of practice. There's no doubt that becoming a good journalist takes an enormous expenditure of time and effort. "Do the work," no matter how tedious, was Bryan Gruley's mantra when he wrote long features for Bloomberg Businessweek magazine and now as the author of thriller fiction.

Without the right attitude and the willingness to make that commitment, the chances of success are slim to none.

ATTITUDE PAYS OFF

David Maraniss is a Pulitzer Prize–winning journalist, best-selling author and associate editor of The Washington Post. But what I remember best about him was what he had to say when I interviewed him after he won a $10,000 American Society of Newspaper Editors award for deadline reporting.

His prize-winning 1996 story—about returning the bodies of government officials killed in a plane crash to Dover Air Force Base—was a stunning meditation on fate and loss reported and written in a matter of hours.

The weather was cold and miserable. Maraniss wound up with pneumonia. But he covered the story like an eager intern.

GIVE AND GET

Maraniss often devoted months to investigations and series. But when news broke, he was one of the first to pitch in.

"Usually when there's some kind of major event happening, I either volunteer to help out, or they ask me," he told me. "Even if I'm doing a series, I say, 'Look, if you guys need me, I'd be happy to do something.' I try to be in a position to say yes..."

He continued, "So many reporters keep banging away at their editors and having frustrating confrontations about what they have to do or don't have to do. I've always found it much more effective to do what I want to do by doing some things for them. There's a fair exchange."

In a field where so much—success and rejection, for starters—is out of a journalist's hands, attitude is one thing we can control. We can decide whether to offer help, as Maraniss did, to procrastinate or commit to one more revision: to learn from others, rather than be consumed by jealousy about their achievements.

AN ATTITUDE CHECKLIST

- Attitude makes the difference between giving up and sticking with a story.
- Attitude means making one more phone call, writing one more draft, burrowing into your story one more time to refine and polish it.
- Attitude means fostering a collaborative relationship with editors rather than a toxic one.

In the end, attitude is what makes the difference between failure and spectacular success.

#3: Letting Objectivity Reign

Let's dispense with this from the start. Objectivity in journalism is a myth. And a dangerous one at that.

Objectivity—journalism free from bias and favoritism—is a lofty goal. But it's an unreachable one.

Oh, you'll hear the opposite, from readers, viewers, editors, teachers and colleagues. "A journalist must remain objective," they insist. That's true if it means that you shouldn't inject your personal opinions into your stories, a restriction younger journalists wrestle with and sometimes reject. Those attitudes belong in editorials or opinion columns, though they too should be buttressed by facts—not fantasy.

THE PYRAMID EFFECT

Any decision a journalist makes is informed by their biases, preferences and experiences. Newsgathering is a series of personal judgment calls about what's important.

The concept of objectivity has been around since the nineteenth century and hotly debated since the early twentieth century.

Today, "neutral 'objective journalism' is constructed atop a pyramid of subjective decision-making," says Wesley Lowery, a Pulitzer Prize-winning reporter and correspondent for CBS News "60 Minutes's" "60 in 6."

The journalist, he wrote in The New York Times in 2020, must choose which stories to cover, which sources to seek out and include and which information to highlight or downplay.

"No journalistic process is objective," Lowery concluded. "And no individual journalist is objective, because no human being is."

WARNING: HAZARD AHEAD

Journalists may approach their work subjectively, but that doesn't make their pursuit of truth any less important or meaningful.

"The concept of objectivity has partly managed to replace a more fundamental one, that of truth," according to a 2012 study published in Journalism Studies.

Objectivity makes us "passive recipients of news, rather than aggressive analyzers and explainers of it," Brent Cunningham, managing editor of Columbia Journalism Review, wrote in 2003.

Journalists chose the latter option in January 2017, when Press Secretary Sean Spicer falsely claimed that attendance at President Donald J. Trump's inauguration was the largest in history. They compared aerial photos and subway ridership in Washington, DC, to prove that Spicer wasn't telling the truth.

Spicer later regretted his actions. "If you ask me for one thing that I probably want a do-over on, that's it," he told National Public Radio in 2018, after he left the White House.

SEARCH FOR TRUTH

Journalists routinely practice the art of selection.

Say you're assigned to write about the hour-long Governor's State of the State message in 500 words or 30 seconds for broadcast. You can't cover every word she says.

"You're always winnowing and chopping and reordering and reassembling the event," Melvin Mencher, my professor at the Columbia University Graduate School of Journalism, reminded me recently.

We may not be capable of objectivity, but we must be open to discovering the story that should be told—not the one we want to tell. There is only one side for journalists to take: the search for the truth wherever it leads, without fear or favor.

To reach that goal, Lowery recommends:

1. Seek perspectives of those you disagree with.
2. Ask tough questions of those you agree with.

So jettison objectivity from your journalistic vocabulary. Replace it with accuracy, fairness and verifiable facts.

#4: Unforced Errors

Have you ever appeared in a newspaper and found your name was misspelled? Maybe it was a friend or family member whose name was botched.

Errors like this are infuriating. Even heartbreaking, especially when the mistake occurs in an obituary. That's the only time most people will ever appear in the news. Loved ones post these stories of life and death in the family Bible, a picture frame, even on the fridge, to keep memories alive.

CREDIBILITY IS THE PRODUCT

A misspelling isn't just a mistake. Such errors damage the essential trust between you and your audience. If you can't get the little things right, people say, why should they trust you with the big things you report?

The product that news organizations sell isn't a newspaper, news show or even advertising. It's credibility. That's even more true in the digital age, when anyone with a computer and an internet hookup can be a publisher, when opinions masquerading as truth zip around social media and politicians and talk show hosts debate the existence of facts.

A RECIPE FOR MISTAKES

Drastic cuts in newsroom staffs, especially editors, and consolidation of responsibilities increase the chance of mistakes.

Shifting the jobs of copyediting and designing pages for the Winston-Salem (North Carolina) Journal to a consolidated editing and design center 70 miles away troubled managing editor Ken Otterbourg so much that it was one of the reasons he quit in 2010, according to a 2013 case study published by The Poynter Institute. The approach, he believed, disconnected those journalists from the communities they were supposed to serve.

"I didn't think it was good for our paper," said Otterbourg. "There's nothing more to it than saving money."

Management defended the practice. But the study noted that, while its journalists "are supposed to catch obvious misspellings, it's not their job to research the names of individuals, streets or companies to confirm obscure spellings." That's a recipe for a correction and a dip in reader confidence.

No one is perfect, of course. The best journalists I know are terrified of making mistakes—"error terror," one calls it. Getting it right is a high-wire act.

"How do you sift through the rumors, the gossip, the failed memories, the manipulative agendas, and try to capture something as accurately as possible, subject to revision in light of new information and perspective?" Bill Kovach and Tom Rosenstiel ask in "The Elements of Journalism." "These are the real questions faced daily by those who try to gather news, understand it, and convey it to others."

"Mistakes happen because we're humans," Ellen E. Clarke, deputy editor for life & culture at the Tampa Bay Times, told the paper's subscribers in an email. "Spellcheck helps, but isn't likely to catch an incorrect tense or words that got jumbled during an edit. Do we hate it? Yes! Can I promise it will never happen again? I sure can't."

WHY MISTAKES ARE MADE

Editors at The Oregonian tracked why their staff made errors. The three most frequent reasons:

1. Working from memory
2. Making assumptions
3. Dealing with second-hand sources

The solution, Kovach and Rosenstiel say, is to adopt accuracy checklists, which include reminders of the most common errors to check for, such as numerical mistakes (See #10 Numbers Don't Add Up), misspelled names and incorrect dates. National Public Radio has the most comprehensive one.

CANCEL ERROR TERROR

- Triple-check every fact in your story—names, ages, addresses, statistics, quotes, etc.—against your notes or public records. "The discipline of verification," Kovach and Rosenstiel say, is "the essential process of arriving as nearly as possible at the truth of the matter at hand." They call it "the beating heart of credible journalism in the public interest."
- Log your efforts. Pulitzer Prize–winner and author Thomas French routinely puts a red checkmark over every fact in his stories, some of them thousands of

words long, to show he'd compared it against his documentation.

- Verify. If you're describing a business transaction, a scientific breakthrough or how a municipal bond works, there's nothing wrong with calling your sources back if you're confused. Read them what you've written. They'll not only set you straight, French found, they often gave him even richer information.

#5: Letting Fear Stop You

"If you want to be a reporter," my journalism teacher said in class one day, "you have to be counterphobic" and he moved on with his lecture.

My hand shot up. "What does counterphobic mean?"

"Do," he said, "what you fear. "

Professor Mencher had struck a nerve.

Before journalism school, my only professional experience consisted of a year on a tiny daily. I had a problem interviewing people, whether they were hostile police officers, perfect strangers at Town Council meetings or neighborhood residents.

I was scared of rebuffs and rejection, of doors slammed in my face and angry shouts of "Beat it!" Even physical violence. (I had an active imagination.)

YOU'RE NOT ALONE

Later, as a journalism teacher and writing coach, I learned that my students and even working journalists feel similar emotions. Fear —of harsh rejection and failure—persists.

"It would astound you to know how many reporters, whose job it is to talk to people, are painfully, horrifically shy," Monica Hesse, a Washington Post columnist, tweeted from a presidential campaign trail. "I'm here in New Hampshire and I get to eat one M&M every time I successfully interview another human."

PEOPLE FEAR YOU MORE

What may help is knowing that many people are actually frightened of journalists.

They fear the 2 E's associated with appearing in the news:

1. **Embarrassment**. People fear being humiliated by their comments, grammar or appearance in a published story.
2. **Exposure**. Some people prefer to remain private, especially when our polarized society may rain down criticism, and even death threats, on social media if they express their beliefs.

HOW TO FIGHT THE FEAR

One other E, **Empathy**—understanding the power you wield— can keep fear from stopping you.

"I carry a can of pepper spray, a Glock pistol and 51 rounds of ammunition," J. C. McKinnon, a gruff St. Petersburg police officer, told my students. "But you've got something that can destroy me: a pen and a notepad."

As a journalist in a democracy, you have the absolute right to approach someone for an interview. Bear in mind that people have the right to say no, but don't let that deter you. Try someone else. Be unfailingly polite and genuinely interested. Most people love to talk about themselves.

Here are four ways you can calm your nerves:

1. Deep breathing exercises calm the body and the mind.
2. Exercise and a hot shower flood the brain with endorphins—the "happy hormone."
3. Chamomile tea soothes a troubled spirit, a journalism friend says.
4. Acknowledge that you're afraid and then do it anyway. Do what you fear.

Journalism takes courage. To write a story that may offend someone, even though it's accurate. To approach complete strangers, sometimes with difficult questions.

"It's all about one thing," a savvy editor once said in a seminar. "Gulp. And go."

#6: Distrusting The Process

Growing up, I thought writers were magicians and I was in trouble because I knew I wasn't.

Writing a news story as a cub reporter felt like hacking my way through a jungle. Panicked, sweaty, I flipped through my notes and flailed away at the keyboard, desperate to make deadline and convinced I wouldn't. I kept my editors waiting, which frustrated them, but they got my copy eventually, flawed though it was, and it made it into the paper. It was a painful process without any clear direction behind it.

As the years passed, not much changed until one day in 1981, when Donald M. Murray was hired as the writing coach at the Providence (Rhode Island) Journal-Bulletin, where I had gotten a job after journalism school.

"Writing may be magical," he told us at the first workshop, "but it's not magic."

I sat up straight and started scribbling in my notebook as he went on. "It's a process, a rational series of decisions you make and steps you take, whatever the assignment, length or deadline," said

Murray, a Pulitzer Prize winner who taught journalism at the University of New Hampshire.

That lesson was the most important element of my education as a writer. I didn't have to be a magician after all.

By following the steps that produce effective writing, you can diagnose and solve your writing problems. Reporters and editors who share a common view and vocabulary become collaborators rather than adversaries.

THE WRITING PROCESS: STEP BY STEP

1. IDEA

Good journalists get assignments or come up with their own ideas. Editors expect enterprise and rely on reporters to see stories that others don't.

Tip

Look for ideas in your newspaper and others. Look online, in social media and in discussion boards. Ask yourself, What would I want to read about? Ask people you meet what's missing in your paper, in your broadcast or on your website.

2. REPORT

Collect specific, accurate information. Not just who, what, when, where, and why, but how. What did it look like? What sounds echoed? What scents lingered in the air? Don't be stingy with your reporting. (See #8 Iceberg Right Ahead!)

Tip

Look for revealing details. "In a good story," says David Finkel of The Washington Post, "a paranoid schizophrenic doesn't just hear imaginary voices, he hears them say, 'Go kill a policeman.'" Use the five senses in your reporting and a few other elements: place, people, time, drama.

3. FOCUS

Confronted with a wealth of reporting, journalists can get lost in the weeds, as I did. Good stories contain a theme—best expressed in one word, like loss or corruption—that leaves a single, dominant impression. Everything in the story must support it.

Tip

What's the news? What's the story? What does it say about life, about the world, about the times we live in? What is it *really* about—in a single word? Your answers will point you forward, frame your story and tell your audience why it matters.

4. ORGANIZE

Generals wouldn't go into battle without a plan. Builders wouldn't lay a foundation without a blueprint in hand. Yet organizing information into coherent, appropriate structures is an overlooked activity for all too many journalists.

Tip

Make a list of the top five elements you want to include. Number them in order of importance. Structure your story accordingly. Or, organize to build dramatic tension. Identify the beginning, an introduction of a problem or challenge. Then establish the middle, where conflict increases. Finally, establish the ending, a climax and resolution to the conflict.

5. DRAFT

Discover by writing, learning what you know and need to know. Freewrite your first draft without your notes. Go back and fill in the blanks.

Tip

Pulitzer Prize–winner Lane DeGregory stashes her notes in her car before writing. "The story isn't in your notebooks," she says. "It's in your head. And heart."

6. REVISE

Circle back to re-report, re-focus and reorganize. Good writers are never content. Find better details, a sharper focus, a beginning that captivates and an ending that leaves a lasting impression.

Tip

Role-play the reader. Does the lead make you want to keep reading? Did you spend too long learning what the story is about and why it's important? What questions do you have about the story? Are they answered in the order you would logically ask them? Cut, move, add.

Trust the process. The magic will happen.

#7: Stumbling On The Steps Of Effective Interviewing

Every day, journalists pick up the phone or head out of the newsroom. They meet a stranger or a familiar contact. They take out a notebook or turn on a recorder. They ask a question and listen to the answer.

Interviewing lies at the heart of journalism. It's a critical path to building an information base that produces fair, complete and accurate stories. Yet few journalists receive education or training in this critical skill and rely on on-the-job training.

"Young journalists still learn by overhearing experienced colleagues conduct master classes in the art of the interview," said Mark Katches, editor of the Tampa Bay Times.

For most, the only way to learn is on the job, often through painful trial and error.

INTERVIEWING STEP-BY-STEP

How do you approach strangers and ask them questions? How do you get people to give you useful answers? How do you use quotes effectively in your stories?

1. Get smart

Want to flop as an interviewer? Don't prepare.

To succeed, research your subject or topic. When former New York Times reporter Mirta Ojito interviewed experts, she said, "I try to know almost as much as they do about their subject, so it seems we are chatting."

2. Craft your questions

The best questions are open-ended: "How?" "What?" "Why?" Conversation starters deliver an abundance of information.

Closed-ended questions are limited, but have an important purpose. Ask them when you need a direct answer. "Did you embezzle the pension fund?" "Are you a member of the Proud Boys?" They put people on the record.

Double-barreled questions are guaranteed to stop conversations. "Why did the campus police use pepper spray on student protesters? Who gave the order?" Double-barreled questions allow sources to avoid the question they want to ignore.

Craft questions in advance. Stick to the script. Ask one question at a time. Don't be afraid to edit yourself. I've stopped myself in the middle of a poorly phrased question and said, "That's a terrible question. Let me put it another way."

3. Listen

"Silence opens the door to hearing dialogue, rare and valuable in breaking stories," says Brady Dennis of The Washington Post. (See #19 Failing to Listen).

4. Empathize

Show sources you have some understanding of their situation. "Interviewing is the modest immediate science of gaining trust, then gaining information," John Brady wrote in "The Craft of Interviewing."

5. Look around

Good interviewers do more than listen.

"I always try to see people at home," said the late Rhode Island journalist Carol McCabe, who filled her stories with rich detail. "I can learn something from where the TV is, whether the set of encyclopedias or bowling trophies is prominently displayed, whether the guy hugs his wife or touches his kids, what's on the refrigerator door." Weave in such details for a richer story.

6. Establish ground rules

You've just finished a great interview when, suddenly, the source says, "Oh, but that's all off the record."

That's the time to point out that there's no such thing as retroactive off the record. Make sure the person you're interviewing knows the score right away. Know the rules. You may have to educate your source, especially if they've never been interviewed by a journalist.

On the record means you can use any information a source tells you and attribute it to the speaker. Sources should assume they're on the record when talking with a journalist, though people inexperienced with the process may need to be taught that.

Off the record means you can't print or broadcast the information or identify the speaker.

On background, also known as "not for attribution," means you can print the quote, but can't identify the source or only do it in a general way that refers to their position—"a source close to the investigation said."

When a source wants to go off the record, stop and ask, "What do you mean?" Try reading back off-the-record comments to a source. Once they hear them, some will change their mind and let you use what they said.

7. Be a lab rat

Record your interviews. Off deadline, transcribe every question and answer verbatim. A recording won't just ensure accurate quotes. It can also be a powerful learning tool. Do you ask more conversation stoppers than starters? Do you step on your subject's words just as they're beginning to open up? Do you sound like a caring, interested human being, or a badgering prosecutor? Study yourself and let your failures—and victories—lead you to rich conversations and richer stories.

#8: Iceberg Right Ahead!

When a lookout on the Titanic sounded the alarm, "Iceberg right ahead," on April 14, 1912, what he feared was not the jagged tops of ice that broke the surface of the North Atlantic, but the mountain beneath. That's because only about one-tenth of an iceberg pierces the water's surface.

The same principle—the theory of omission, or what Ernest Hemingway called "the iceberg" theory—holds true in news writing.

Effective journalists always gather more information than they need. By the time you've finished a 15-inch story or a 60-second broadcast package, you may have interviewed half a dozen people and pored over a stack of background materials, including sheaves of reports, press releases, statements, and screenfuls of internet research.

Too often, we sink our stories with information we can't bear to part with, even if it's not relevant. "But I spent two hours interviewing the Assistant Under-Secretary of State for Non-Essential Information," we wail. "I need four paragraphs to describe that room."

When our editor says, "keep it short," or the copy desk sends word to "trim by a third," we moan, "I don't know what to cut. It's all great stuff."

Stephen Buckley, who shone as a foreign correspondent for The Washington Post, told me, "I always worry that I don't have enough material for a story, so I overreport. Of course, then I have so much to wade through."

"You can't ever overdo it," I replied. "You can't overreport or research too much. But you can under think. You can under plan. You can under revise."

WHAT LIES BENEATH

What makes a powerful story is all the work that lies beneath. It isn't wasted effort, as many journalists fear, but instead constitutes the essential component that gives writing its greatest power: making every word count.

Writers write best with an overabundance of material, as my mentor, Don Murray, taught me.

Alix Freedman always kept in mind her Wall Street Journal editor's description of journalism's essential challenge: "Distill a beer keg's worth of information into a perfume bottle."

That's why the Pulitzer Prize-winning investigative reporter cataloged her reporting on a legal pad where she listed quotes, examples, statistics and themes she uncovered in her reporting.

Each got a grade. Only those marked "A" made it into print. Freedman's aim was to "maximize impact," to use "not just an example but a telling example," she said. Not just a quote but "a quote on point."

The power of a story comes from what's not in it.

It's a paradox, one of many contradictions that lie in the journalist's path.

But you ignore it at your peril.

UNLOADING TIPS

Copy Alix Freedman's approach. List your reporting elements, grade them and only use the ones you give a top grade to.

Read your story aloud. You'll hear where it sinks under the weight of your material.

Slash away. If you've done enough reporting, you can cut entire passages and paragraphs without losing the story's heft, rather than hunting for single words to trim.

#9: Bloated Quotes

Get out one of your stories and start counting. Not all the words, just the ones between quotation marks.

Chances are you'll get quite a mouthful.

We all know the importance of avoiding run-on sentences in our copy, but too often our standards drop when those twin apostrophes enter the picture, and we end up with quotes that run off at the mouth.

PUT YOUR QUOTES ON A DIET

The value of quote reduction became evident when I asked bureau reporters at a metropolitan daily paper to add up the quotes in their stories. Many quotes weighed in at 30–40 words, with some tipping the scale at 40–50 and even higher.

Reporters were all too often using quotes as filler, bulking up a journalistic meal with the empty calories of verbiage.

Bloated quotes are an easy trap to fall into when people—especially politicians, bureaucrats and lawyers—talk as if they're billing by the word.

A 45–60 word jargon-ridden quote explaining a sewer bond proposal may seem like an easy solution for the writer. But it can choke a reader, making comprehension difficult as the brain struggles to process the information.

Many reporters use quotations as a crutch. They forget that they, not their sources, are writing the story. Obviously, there are times when it's important we get the news directly from the source. No paraphrase would have had the impact of President Bill Clinton's 1998 declaration, "I did not have sexual relations with that woman, Miss Lewinsky." Clinton said more that day about his relationship with the young White House intern, but this 11-word quote is the one that people remember.

By all means, fill your stories with voices, but just as you'd steer clear of a windbag at a party, spare your readers those bloated quotes that deaden a piece of writing.

1. Take 10 percent off the top. Trim the fat, leaving a verbatim message, and paraphrase the rest.

2. Punctuate with quotes. Use quotes to drive home a point at the end of a paragraph.

3. Stay tuned for echoes. Notice how many stories contain quotes that repeat what has already been written. "Mayor Foghorn said he's pleased with the election results, noting that his victory demonstrates his popularity with the voters. "I'm pleased with the results," the mayor said. "It proves my popularity with the voters." Readers don't need a paraphrase and a quote with the same information to understand. One or the other will suffice.

4. Listen. Keep your quotes lean by reading your story aloud as you make final revisions. Reserve quotation marks for words that reveal character, advance the narrative or drive home a controversial point. Don't use every quote in your notebook to prove you did the interviews. That's not writing. It's dictation.

5. Follow the one-breath rule. If a quote takes more than one breath to read, it's too long. If you've got a good quote that takes more than one breath, insert attribution in the middle. It will make comprehension easier for the reader.

6. Harness paraphrases. Unless a source can say it better than you, paraphrase it. You're the writer, after all. A well-constructed paraphrase accurately summing up a remark, and punctuated with a brief quote, adds a powerful punch.

A great quote is like a butterfly snatched from the air. It's quick and flashy. Shoot for between six and 20 words to keep the reader engaged.

#10: Numbers Don't Add Up

In school, I hated numbers and loved words. My verbal skills propelled me into journalism, where math didn't matter.

Or so I thought.

When city officials raised property taxes, I needed to calculate a percentage rate on deadline. A press release, which reported statistics behind a new study, needed critical analysis to ensure that they supported the findings. A person's age or a phone number for an event had to be reported accurately.

Numbers in news stories—stock prices, inflation rates, city budgets, dates, ages and addresses—abound. But all too often, careless or unskilled reporters and editors let inaccurate ones make their way into the news, says investigative reporter David Cay Johnston, who cataloged common mistakes:

- Millions confused with billions and trillions.
- Misplaced decimal points.
- Assuming statistics in official announcements are correct when they "are often rich with math errors."

INNUMERATES RULE

There's no room for illiterates in a newsroom, but innumerates—defined by mathematician John Allen Paulos as those uncomfortable with fundamental notions of numbers and the possibilities of things happening by chance—are everywhere.

Math leaves some journalists feeling terrified. They'll accept figures from a source or a press release without trying to verify them.

Getting numbers wrong about diseases or accidents can leave readers frightened without reason by journalistic hyperbole and open to fraudulent schemes. The profession's most serious numeracy failing, journalism professor Scott Maier asserts, citing "A Mathematician Reads the Newspaper" by Paulos, is "neither statistical ignorance nor blunder but a lack of appreciation of how mathematics can be used to sharpen and broaden the view of the world."

Journalism is crowded with math-phobes who told their professors, "If I wanted to do math, I wouldn't have majored in journalism." The result is a cascade of botched numbers and numerical errors that rank among the most common mistakes made by journalists, according to Craig Silverman, whose book "Regret the Error" uses corrections to document the causes and effects of journalistic mistakes.

Two examples:

- "How to... improve your swimming," a story in the British newspaper The Guardian, had this advice: Find a pool "heated" to 28 degrees Fahrenheit. The correction that followed noted that that temperature was below freezing. What they meant to say was 28 Celsius (82F).
- The Wall Street Journal issued a correction for a recipe for a Bloody Mary mix after it transposed the amount of

vodka and tomato juice, calling for 12 ounces of juice and 36 ounces of booze.

Readers and viewers notice when your numbers don't add up.

Maier, a University of Oregon journalism professor, surveyed 1,000 sources who appeared in the Raleigh (North Carolina) News & Observer. They identified "an average of two stories with numerical errors in each newspaper edition," according to his study, published in Newspaper Research Journal. "What appears to be lacking," Maier wrote, "is a willingness to question numbers that don't make sense."

THREE PATHS TO FAILURE

Numerical errors come in three major categories, says Silverman:

1. Miscalculations or interpretations made by a reporter.
2. A typographical error that misplaces a decimal point, adds a zero or garbles a phone number or date.
3. Figures provided by a third party and passed on by the media without proper vetting.

WRITING WITH NUMBERS

Words, not data, make a story. Put your verbal skills to work at conveying data without putting people to sleep.

- **Comparison-shop**. Put a figure in context by comparing it to something else that people can grasp. "To store a gigabyte's worth of data just 20 years ago required a refrigerator-sized machine weighing 500 pounds," IBM says on its website. "Today, that same gigabyte's worth of data resides comfortably on a disk smaller than a coin."

- **Round off and substitute**. Economists and financial experts need exact numbers. Readers don't. If 33 percent of the drivers in fatal crashes had alcohol in their blood, it would be clearer if you say, "One in three drivers had been drinking."

BANISH YOUR MATH-PHOBIA

1. You don't have to be a math whiz to succeed and serve up accurate stories for your audience. Often, simple arithmetic, a calculator and close attention to detail can prevent the most common mistakes. You can also find math resources, including percentage change and interest rate calculators, online.
2. Don't be afraid to run your numbers by your source before you publish for accuracy, not censoring. Or to challenge them, if necessary.
3. Find a math-savvy colleague or friend to review your figures before you submit your story.
4. Keep crib sheets—formulas for how to determine percentages, rates, etc.—close at hand as you work with numbers.
5. Go back to school, using online resources designed to teach journalists how to do math.
6. Check the numbers that crop up in your reporting against other values, such as inflation rates and other historical figures. The comparisons you make will give you context for understanding numbers better and may reveal previously unnoticed issues.

#11: Bothsidesism

"I want to get both sides of the story." That's a line reporters often use to get a comment on an issue under debate. You've probably used it yourself to try to convince sources to cooperate.

The sentiment sounds fair, but it can lead to false balance, which gives unsupported points of view the aura of truth and equal time in news stories. Call it, as some do, "bothsidesism."

The problem reflects an "ingrained journalistic habit that tries mightily to avoid any hint of reporting bias," conservative scholar Norm Ornstein wrote in The Atlantic. "The reflexive 'we report both sides of every story,' even to the point that one side is given equal weight not supported by reality."

WHEN TWO SIDES TAKE CENTER STAGE

Consider climate change.

Since the early 2000s, a consensus has existed in the scientific community that global warming is a human-made phenomenon, caused by burning fossil fuels.

Yet a minority of voices—academics, scientists, politicians and business people, known as "climate contrarians" who reject that conclusion— were featured in 49 percent more media articles than climate scientists between 2000 and 2016, according to a 2019 study in Nature Communications.

Considerable column inches and air time were also devoted in 2003 to those who maintained that the MMR (measles, mumps and rubella) vaccine given to infants and children caused autism, even though a study in the British Medical Journal reported that "almost all scientific experts rejected the claim of a link."

By then, however, "most people wrongly believed that doctors and scientists" were equally divided over the vaccine's safety, the study found. More than half of those surveyed assumed that because both sides of the debate received equal media coverage, there must be equal evidence for each.

An anti-vaccine movement, which thrives in today's Covid-19 pandemic, was born.

Getting both sides of a story may sound like the fair approach, but in the end, false balance, at the expense of truth, can deceive the public and is a prime factor behind the partisan divide that has split America. Bothsidesism can lead to headlines that give even more unearned credence to views with little evidence, which are then circulated widely on social media.

FIGHTING BACK

- Assess the evidence presented by all sides. Checking doesn't necessarily mean including every point of view in the story, but recognizing false balance should be a vital part of the reporting process.
- Newsworthy examples, like the 2022 Canadian trucker "Freedom Convoy" protest against vaccine mandates,

must be covered, but put in context—organizers included far-right activists—and not sensationalized. If a point of view isn't solid, resist the impulse to include it, or, as the media generally does with former President Donald J. Trump's assertion that the 2020 election was stolen from him, identify it as unsupported by the facts.

#12: Tuning In USUCK FM

You're ready to write. Coffee steams on your desk. The computer hums. Inspiration awaits. You lower your fingers to the keys.

Then you hear it. A whisper in your ear.

"You suck."

What's that? Where did that come from?

"You suck!" it repeats. The hiss is louder.

Wait a minute. It's coming from inside your head.

"You can't write. You're a loser."

I used to think it was just me, a profane ex–newspaper reporter, whose potty mouth delivered this warning.

After years leading writing seminars and coaching hundreds of writers, however, I discovered I was not alone. An editor at the Los Angeles Times heard it so often, she said it was like a radio station—I named it USUCK FM—playing inside her head all day long. Writers all over, including some whose names will surprise you, hear the same negative refrain.

"I'm afraid of failing at whatever story I'm writing—that it won't come up for me, or that I won't be able to finish it." That's Stephen King. Yes, *that* Stephen King.

Mental health experts have another name for this playlist of insecurity: impostor phenomenom. In 1978, psychologists Pauline Rose Clance and Suzanne Ament Imes introduced the term to describe a persistent belief among sufferers that "they are really not bright and have fooled anyone who thinks otherwise." It afflicts not just successful and struggling writers, but luminaries such as astronaut Neil Armstrong, Oscar-winning actor Tom Hanks and former First Lady Michelle Obama. So, if you feel like a fraud, join this select club.

LOWER YOUR STANDARDS

William Stafford never heard the voice of self-doubt. He woke up before dawn every day and wrote. Before he died in 1993, at the age of 79, he had written thousands of poems and published scores of books. He was never blocked because he located the transmitter for USUCK FM: impossibly high standards.

"One should lower his standards until there is no felt threshold to go over in writing," Stafford says in "Writing the Australian Crawl." "It's easy to write. You just shouldn't have standards that inhibit you from writing."

I've come to believe in Stafford's counsel so much that I don't just lower my standards. I abandon them. I allow myself to write as badly as I can. You can do the same.

At first.

Drafting is where you discover your story, your voice, your characters, the building blocks that will erect the edifice of your reporting, your language skills and imagination.

After that, you have to be your toughest critic, making sure your news story is accurate, fair and properly balanced, that the names, ages, facts, spelling and grammar are triple-checked. That your characters are full-bodied, the structure elegant, the conflict established from the start and the climax stunning. That's what revision is for. But that assessment comes after you've written.

FREEWRITE YOUR WAY TO FLUENCY

Lowering your standards is a good idea—in theory. But how do you apply it? Freewriting is a writing strategy popularized by Peter Elbow, who believes that writing calls on "two skills that are so different that they usually conflict with each other: creating and criticizing," as he wrote in "Writing with Power." They need to operate separately. Otherwise, writer's block ensues.

The solution?

"Just start typing and don't stop," says Sree Sreenivasan, a digital media expert at Arizona State University's Walter Cronkite School of Journalism and Mass Communication who has embraced the practice. "Keep going without hitting the backspace even if you make errors. This opens your mind and forces you to get something down. You can always rewrite."

Your inner critic may be screaming, "Stop!" but pay no mind. The trick is to type so fast that the clacking of the keys drowns out that voice.

At first, free writes aren't very focused. "I have no ideas or energy, " you may begin. "Not a clue what to say." But persist, even for just 10–15 minutes, and USUCK FM switches off. You will write faster. Agonize less. Have more time for revision. Publish more.

Type so fast that you can slip past the DJ at USUCK FM before he has time to cry out, "Hey, you, get back here! You suck!"

#13: Revision Rejection

Journalists spend most of their time reporting. That's their job, after all. Then, as the clock ticks toward deadline, they start banging away at their keyboard, desperately trying to compose a coherent story.

Revision? Heck, they'd tell you, I'm just trying to get the darn thing written. And if I turn it in late enough, the editors can't tamper with my flawless prose.

Journalism is essentially a first-draft culture, and therein lies the problem. Until you overcome resistance to revision and start seeing it as the chance to improve your stories, your readers will find it easy to quit reading.

Granted, sometimes there isn't time for anything but a first draft. But just because journalism has been called "the first rough draft of history" shouldn't give writers—and their editors—an excuse to publish hastily edited first drafts every time.

A POP QUIZ

When I hear the word *revision*, I think...

1. I should have gotten it right the first time.
2. I have no clue how to revise my story.
3. I don't have the time.
4. Yippee! I've got another chance to make it right.

Revision is the key to making a story shine, but not many working and student journalists I've coached choose number 4. Instead, they beat themselves up with the first three responses.

Revision—literally to "re-see"—gives the writer the opportunity to reconsider, reorganize and rewrite until the story reflects an acute clarity.

It shouldn't be confused with proofreading, the final step before publication that examines the story to correct typos, misspellings, and punctuation mistakes.

The biggest problem with revising is not the words, it's the attitude.

As a young journalist, I used to hate the idea of revision. If I were smarter, I told myself, I'd get it right the first time. If I were really talented, my writing would emerge fully formed; no chrysalis but a beautiful butterfly. An engaging lead, logical transitions that drew in the reader and a resonant ending. A home run on the first pitch.

If I had to rewrite my story, it meant one thing: I've failed.

But over the years, I've had a change of heart, and you can too.

I am inspired by writers such as the acclaimed novelist Toni Morrison, who said "the best part of all, the absolutely most delicious part, is finishing it and then doing it over. I rewrite a lot, over and over again, so that it looks like I never did."

Treat revision not as punishment, but as an opportunity for each draft to teach you how to write the next one. "Revision," as Rosalind Bentley, a features/enterprise reporter at the Atlanta Journal-Constitution, told me, "is your friend."

REVISION STRATEGIES

1. **Write earlier**. This teaches you what you already know and what you need to know and builds revision into the process sooner.

2. **Hit the print button**. Computers are awesome, but they give the illusion of perfection. Shifting to another medium using a printer the old-fashioned way will give you the distance you need to see your story in a new light. Mark it up: "cut?" "move up?" "boring?" "stronger evidence?" Quickly make the changes on your computer. If there's something you don't know how to fix, move on. In the next version, the problem may have vanished. If not, cut it. Repeat the process as many times before deadline.

3. **Put it away.** Take a walk around the block. Chat with a colleague in the break room. Any attempt to put a story out of your mind, however brief, will give your mind the chance to work on it.

4. **Read it aloud.** Listen to your story and you can hear where it lags, where a quote runs on or echoes the previous phrase.

5. **Find a beta reader**. Before you turn in your story, ask a friend or colleague to look at it. Ask them to tell you what works and what needs work.

6. **Develop patience**. When we begin to write, ideas often flow in a flood. Instead of a tidy piece of prose, what you have is a mess

that makes your spirits droop. Keep telling yourself excellence will come, if you keep at it.

#14: Missing Multimedia

When he began his journalism career in the 1970s, the only thing Peter Bhatia carried to assignments was a notebook slim enough to fit into his jacket pocket and a pencil with a good eraser.

Bhatia doesn't wax nostalgic about the past, though. As editor of the Detroit Free Press, he marvels when one of his reporters livestreams video from a football game in Michigan Stadium to freep.com, the paper's website. "That was unimaginable," he told me.

Multimedia is a driving force behind revenues today as news organizations struggle to attract eyeballs and digital subscriptions to stay afloat. They depend on their journalists to deliver that content.

A smartphone, with its phone, audio recorder and still and video camera features, has become the essential tool to get the job done. And these devices aren't capturing the grainy, low frame rate footage of first-generation smartphones. Newer models have begun to rival the image quality of much larger—and more expensive—professional cameras.

Storytelling remains the heart of great journalism, and multimedia provides new ways to convey and enhance the written word. It also gives reporters a means to bring audiences breaking news coverage in real time.

Journalists who entered the business just to write stories now have to take a "multimedia first" approach to reporting.

MULTIMEDIA CHECKLIST

- **Start capturing video immediately**, whether it's a fire, a festival or a protest.
- **Tweet the story**, keeping your editors apprised, and pause to check for accuracy, misspellings and punctuation errors, just as you would for a print story, before you hit send.
- **Take photos**—both candid action shots that document what you see and posed portraiture of the characters who will appear in your stories.
- **Invest** in some basic accessories—a tripod and phone adapter, a decent pair of headphones, a dedicated audio recorder—for more flexibility in the field.

"If you really want to screw up your story," Bhatia said, "don't have any visuals, don't have any video, don't have any audio. You've got to have those additional elements to pull people in."

#15: Libel Pains

The very word strikes terror in the heart of every journalist.

Libel—publishing false statements that expose someone to public hatred, contempt, or ridicule in writing or pictures—can trigger a costly lawsuit or the possibility of a hefty payout to settle the case. Originally limited to newspapers, it now includes broadcast news on radio, television and online publications. Slander is another form of libel that involves oral communication.

In 2017, Disney, the parent company of ABC News, settled a $1.9 billion libel lawsuit by paying a South Dakota beef production company $177 million. At issue was a 2012 broadcast that described a type of meat filler used in ground beef as ammonia-treated "pink slime," once used only in dog food, according to the broadcast story and news reports. Disney's insurers, the beef company said, paid the remainder of the total undisclosed settlement. The company, which maintained the filler is 100 percent beef, said it lost millions in sales and had to lay off 700 workers.

While such cases get big headlines, the reality is that routine stories that are insufficiently checked are behind most libel actions.

The bar is higher for public officials, and public figures—those who hold no office but are widely known. They must prove that the news organization knew the statement was false and published it anyway, known as "actual malice."

Failure to prove that accusation led a federal jury to reject former GOP vice-presidential candidate Sarah Palin's 2022 lawsuit against The New York Times over an editorial linking her political rhetoric to a mass shooting. The editor in charge acknowledged he moved "too fast," but insisted he didn't act out of malice, just carelessness. The paper immediately put out a correction.

THE ELEMENTS OF LIBEL

To prove they have been libeled by a news organization, according to the Reporters Committee for Freedom of the Press, a person must demonstrate six things:

1. Publication in a newspaper, broadcast, or website.
2. Identification. The person doesn't have to be named if their identity—a local coach, say—is clear.
3. Defamation that exposes a person to hatred and ridicule or injures her business. (Libel suits are often called defamation actions.)
4. False. Were the allegations false? Even an altered or incorrect quote can be false.
5. Fault. Did the publication know the story was false and defamatory and publish it anyway?
6. Injury/ Harm. The heart of a libel action is that the person's reputation suffered injury, stated in dollars.

WINNING CAN HURT, TOO

Even winning a libel suit can be costly.

In 2021, a federal court judge threw out a libel suit clearing Reveal, a nonprofit newsroom run by the Center for Investigative Reporting, from charges that it defamed Planet Aid, an international charity that received federal funds. Reveal's reports linked the charity to an alleged cult and questioned its spending.

"While the judge's decision is an unequivocal legal win for Reveal, it took more than four-and-a-half years and millions of dollars to get there," wrote Reveal's general counsel, D. Victoria Baranetsky, in an article about the case in Columbia Journalism Review.

Frank Greve, an investigative reporter for Knight Ridder Newspapers and a former colleague, beat back a libel suit, but he still called the experience "20 months of acute professional anxiety." In his case, truth, as it is generally, was the best defense against a libel action.

But that doesn't cover everything, as I discovered when Frank shared the lessons he learned with me:

1. The tougher the story, the more generous a reporter should be in allowing its target to have his or her say.
2. Reporting findings is more useful to readers than reporting conclusions. Distinguishing between findings and conclusions is libel insurance.
3. Check all numbers. Check them again. Then get someone else to check them.
4. If the target won't comment, send a letter with your questions well before you publish. Follow up with a phone call. It's impressive evidence of a reporter's intent to be fair.
5. Do some reporting on your sources' motives.

6. Listen to your inner voice that asks incessantly: *Is what I'm writing fair?*

#16: Cut-And-Paste Jobs

Plagiarism, the theft of another writer's words and ideas, is one of journalism's cardinal sins. Ryan Broderick learned that the hard way.

In 2020, he lost his job as senior reporter at the news website BuzzFeed after an investigation determined 11 of his articles had been plagiarized or incorrectly attributed to other sources, according to The Wall Street Journal.

"It is BuzzFeed News' policy that nothing may be copied, pasted, and passed off as one's own work, and that all quotes should be attributed," Buzzfeed's Editor-in-Chief Mark Schoofs wrote readers. "We regret that in these instances those standards were not met."

Journalists had been stealing words before, but the cut-and-paste functions on word processors that emerged in the 1970s have made it a snap to lift another's prose.

At a time when so much research is conducted on the internet, some journalists find the allure of purloined words hard to resist.

You're researching a story on the internet and come across a well-crafted sentence or paragraph that fits your piece perfectly. It's better than anything you have.

IGNORE THE TEMPTATION

You're tempted.

With a few keystrokes, you could easily lift the material and paste it into your story. You can change a few words around, thinking that the theft won't be obvious. Or you come across a lively quote. This time, you pass it off as your own.

"Never plagiarize," the Society of Professional Journalists' Code of Ethics says flat out. Your news organization probably echoes the sentiment in its stylebook.

And remember, the same computer systems that embolden word theft can also be turned on the offender by searching databases for borrowed materials.

The common excuses plagiarists trot out—haste, sloppy note-taking, deadline pressure—won't always save you. Plagiarism can be the equivalent of a career death sentence.

The ethical choice, and one that will protect you from dire punishment: do your own original reporting. If you still want to use another's words directly, attribute them to the source, or paraphrase them and include where the information came from.

There's a simple solution, one that I lay out in my journalism textbook "Reporting and Writing: Basics for the 21st Century": "If you think you should attribute it, then attribute it," says Thomas Mallon, author of "Stolen Words," a history of plagiarism.

"Manage your time wisely," my book continues. "Plagiarism is a desperate act. Writers behind on a deadline, exhausted, anxious, may delude themselves into believing that what they're doing is nothing more than a shortcut. Be honest about where you got your information."

If Ryan Broderick had followed the rule, he'd still have his job.

#17: Making It Up

It seems like a no-brainer—journalists shouldn't make up things in their stories. Tell that to Jayson Blair, Janet Cooke, and Stephen Glass.

They are the most infamous fabulists in modern journalism history. Fabrications cost them not just their jobs, but their careers and tarred their publications.

The fallout at The New York Times, where Blair repeatedly made up quotes, invented scenes and plagiarized other reporters' work, also toppled the paper's top two editors in 2003.

Cooke was an ambitious reporter at The Washington Post when she wrote "Jimmy's World," about an eight-year-old heroin addict. The story won her the Pulitzer Prize in 1981. The only problem: she made Jimmy up. It cost her the prize, her career, and damaged her paper's reputation.

Equally driven, Stephen Glass lost his job in 1998 at The New Republic and a lucrative freelance career when it was discovered that more than 40 of his stories were littered with fictitious characters and made-up quotes.

"We busy, friendly folks were no match for such a willful deceiver," said Charles Lane, who edited some of Glass's stories.

FABRICATION FALLOUT

Making up stories in the news is not a new phenomenon. In 1835, the New York Sun ran a series of sensational articles about life on the moon, which it said was inhabited by "man-bats" and beavers that walked on two feet.

Fabricators are driven by ambition and desperation. They benefit from trusting editors, lax fact-checking and a passion for scoops, reader-friendly stories, and prizes.

They pay the ultimate price that every journalist should keep in mind for violating the cardinal sin of journalism.

At last reports, Blair was a life coach and Glass earned a law degree but, barred from practicing, works as a paralegal. In 2015, Glass repaid Harper's magazine $10,000 for a discredited article; a year later, he told journalism students at Duke University he had paid a total of $200,000 to the publications he had wronged.

Fifteen years after "Jimmy's World," Cooke was working in a department store for $6 an hour, the Post reported in 1996. Writing in Columbia Journalism Review in 2016, author Mike Sager, her former boyfriend at the Post, would say only that "she is living within the borders of the continental United States, within a family setting, and pursuing a career that does not primarily involve writing."

IS PREVENTION POSSIBLE?

The lessons learned from these dispiriting cases, ethics experts said, include more training, newsroom discussions, and what some call "prosecutorial editing," when every fact is scrutinized. A reporter feeling pressure could muster the courage to confide in her editor the stress she feels under.

All that may not be enough, though, when a skilled fabricator decides making it up is easier than doing the hard work of reporting.

#18: Ignoring Your Biases

In April 2018, Rashon Nelson and Donte Robinson walked into a neighborhood Starbucks in Philadelphia. They asked to use the bathroom and declined to make a purchase, explaining that they were waiting for a business associate.

The manager called the police.

In an episode captured on a customer's cellphone, police handcuffed the two men and took them to a police station, where they were charged with trespassing and creating a disturbance.

The two men were Black. The manager was white. The incident sparked protests and sit-ins at Starbucks nationwide. The company's CEO apologized, calling the incident "reprehensible." A month later, the chain closed all of its stores for an afternoon, it said, to give racial-basis training to its nearly 175,000 employees.

THE NATURE OF BIASES

Biases are unsupported, and often unconscious or "implicit," assumptions we make about people and groups that we perceive as different from us. They are a hardwired survival instinct that makes us feel safe only with people like us.

"We all have them," Sewell Chan, editor in chief of The Texas Tribune, told me. "Biases based on where we grew up, how we were raised, what ethnicity, race, religion we belong to; biases based on our gender identity and sexual orientation; many more."

To do your job effectively, you must recognize your biases and not let them affect how you report and write.

If you're straight, you may be biased against gay or transgendered people. If you're a person of color, you may harbor negative attitudes toward whites. You may not realize it.

Russia's 2022 invasion of Ukraine surfaced several examples of bias against non-white refugees. In one instance, Al Jazeera English apologized for presenter Peter Dobbie's on-air description of Ukrainians fleeing the war with Russia as "prosperous, middle-class people" who "are not obviously refugees trying to get away from areas in the Middle East that are still in a big state of war; these are not people trying to get away from areas in North Africa, they look like any European family that you would live next door to." The network called his comments, which were echoed by several other news organizations, "inappropriate, insensitive, and irresponsible" and said disciplinary action would be taken.

The Arab and Middle Eastern Journalists Association condemned this type of commentary, labeling it "explicit bias" that "reflects the pervasive mentality in Western journalism of normalizing tragedy in parts of the world such as the Middle East, Africa, South Asia, and Latin America. It dehumanizes and renders their experience with war as somehow normal and expected."

These are what Malcolm Gladwell in "Blink: The Power of Thinking Without Thinking" calls "the dark side of rapid cognition."

Such split-second responses to a particular group can affect who you interview or feature in your stories and how you characterize them.

"A journalist who fails to recognize she has blind spots can unintentionally distort the meaning of her reporting," Isaac J. Bailey, a journalist who runs race relations seminars, wrote in Nieman Reports.

John Eligon, a reporter for The New York Times, fell into this trap when he wrote a front-page profile of Michael Brown, the 18-year-old Black teen killed in August 2014 by a white police officer in Ferguson, Missouri, prompting nationwide protests. Two words in the fifth paragraph—that Brown was "no angel"— provoked a firestorm on social media and in letters to the editor.

"That choice of words was a regrettable mistake," concluded Margaret Sullivan, the paper's public editor.

Angry readers thought the Times seemed to suggest that Brown was "a bad kid," she wrote, or worse, that "he deserved to die because he acted like many a normal teenager."

Eligon's intent "was likely a sincere attempt to describe Brown's past run-ins with authority and a much-discussed strong-arm robbery as part of a fuller picture of the complex life the teenager had lived," Bailey said. "In the context of the emotional issue of questionable police shootings, to many readers, it signaled something sinister."

"Hindsight is 20/20. I wish I would have changed that," said Eligon, who is Black, and has had unprovoked run-ins with the police as a journalist.

POSTSCRIPT

Starbucks settled with Rashon Nelson and Donte Robinson for an undisclosed amount and an offer of free college tuition at an online university. The city paid each the $1—that's right, one dollar—that they asked for, expunged their arrest records and agreed to fund a $200,000 grant program for aspiring public high school entrepreneurs.

COMBATTING BIAS

1. Take a personal inventory of your biases, reflecting on attitudes you absorbed in your upbringing.
2. Recognize your biases as you approach an interview and seek out diverse sources. Are they all white men? Do you keep a "rainbow" contact list that reflects diverse identities, perspectives and backgrounds?
3. Ask your newsroom leaders to sponsor bias training.
4. Examine your stories closely before publication for any biases that may appear.
5. Spend time with people different from you. "As journalists, we're not omniscient," Chan, The Texas Tribune's editor, said. "It's our job to talk to people different from ourselves, understand them, and explain where they're coming from—in good faith—even, or especially, if that makes us uncomfortable."

#19: Failing To Listen

In the 1976 movie "All the President's Men, " Washington Post reporter Bob Woodward, played by Robert Redford, is on the telephone with a Republican businessman whose $25,000 check has ended up in the money trail of the Watergate scandal that led to President Richard M. Nixon's downfall. Woodward wants to know how. The source is skittish: "I know I shouldn't be telling you this," he says.

Woodward closes his eyes. You can almost hear him praying, "*Tell me, please.*" But he holds his tongue. Suddenly, the man blurts out the damaging truth, implicating a top Nixon campaign official in the cover-up.

The moral: To get people to talk, you need to learn the power of silence and master the art of listening.

LEARN TO LISTEN

Using an audio recorder and transcribing interviews taught me the power of silence the hard way. It hurt to hear me step on people's words, cutting them off just as they were getting enthusiastic or, as Woodward's source did, about to make a revealing statement. My stories suffered, and if you make the same mistakes, yours will too.

Silence makes people uncomfortable. They jump in to fill the void. So it's not surprising that many journalists have a hard time keeping quiet during interviews.

"We don't listen. We just talk, and we talk, and we talk," said Pat Stith, a Pulitzer Prize–winning investigative reporter. "When we're talking, we're not acquiring anything."

Failing to listen means missing out on rich quotes, dialogue, and untold stories that could enrich your piece. You lose the chance, Lane DeGregory of the Tampa Bay Times told me, "to really savor the quiet, note the unanswered questions, and follow the meandering side trips that subjects take you on."

JUST SHUT UP!

For decades, historian Robert A. Caro has been convincing people who knew and worked with the notoriously private President Lyndon B. Johnson to open up.

"When I'm waiting for the person I'm interviewing to break a silence by giving me a piece of information I want," Caro writes in his book "Working" about his reporting methods, "I write 'SU' (for Shut Up!) in my notebook. If anyone were ever to look through my notebooks, he would find a lot of 'SU's.'"

PRACTICE ACTIVE LISTENING

- **Remain silent** after posing a question. If it's difficult, count to 10 inwardly before you ask another one. Follow Robert Caro's "SU" approach.
- **Give nonverbal signals**, like a nod of your head, or a smile, that you're paying attention.

- **Paraphrase** what you've heard—"If I hear you correctly, you believe...")?
- **Show empathy** by being alert to emotional signals—a sigh of resignation or tears—from the source, and then follow up to make sure you understand.

#20: Tripping Ethical Land Mines

Your newsroom has received several complaints about poor conditions at a local nursing home. Its owners refuse to comment and deny your requests to visit the facility to gather firsthand information. Is it proper for a reporter to disguise her identity and apply for a job there to get the story?

You're on deadline, and find online the perfect quote in a rival publication that buttresses your theme. Can you paraphrase that quote without attribution?

An inflammatory story appears on social media. Do you hit Retweet or first wait to research its veracity?

"Journalists travel through moral mine fields," my former Poynter Institute colleagues Bob Steele and Paul Pohlman have written. Among them: Intense deadlines. Competitive fervor. Complex issues. Contradictory facts. All of which add up to an erosion of common sense and good intentions. Many news organizations established ground rules for ethical behavior to deal with, among others, the cases noted above.

1. "No staffer will represent himself or herself as anything other than a Dallas Morning News reporter, editor, photographer, artist, columnist or other occupation."

-Dallas Morning News

2. "Plagiarism is one of journalism's unforgivable sins—and, at this newspaper, a dismissible offense."

-Grand Forks (North Dakota) Herald

3. "The Internet's unique characteristics do not lower the standards by which we evaluate, gather and disseminate information... Material disseminated online should be solidly confirmed."

-Tampa (Florida) Tribune

MAKE SOUND, JUSTIFIABLE ETHICAL DECISIONS

Ethical decision-making is a skill you must practice and master to sidestep these land mines. It often means choosing alternatives that allow you to maximize truth telling while minimizing harm.

Journalists face too many different ethical challenges to be covered by a blanket set of rigid rules.

It's more important, according to the Society of Professional Journalists' Handbook "Doing Ethics in Journalism," that journalists be guided by a set of principles that can aid them in making decisions. They include:

1. Seek truth and report it as fully as possible

- Give voice to the voiceless.
- Hold the powerful accountable.

- Remember that neither speed nor format excuses inaccuracy.
- Identify sources clearly. Consider sources' motives before promising anonymity.
- Never plagiarize. Always attribute.
- Avoid undercover or other surreptitious methods of gathering information unless traditional, open methods will not yield information vital to the public.

2. Act independently

- Guard vigorously the essential stewardship role a free press plays in an open society.
- Remain free of associations and activities that may compromise your integrity or damage your credibility.
- Avoid conflicts of interest, real or perceived.
- Deny favored treatment to advertisers, donors or any other special interests.

3. Minimize harm

- Balance the public's need for information against potential harm or discomfort.
- Be compassionate for those affected by your actions.
- Treat sources, subjects and colleagues as human beings deserving of respect, not merely as means to your journalistic ends.
- Recognize that legal access to information differs from an ethical justification to publish or broadcast.

4. Be accountable and transparent

Ethical journalism means taking responsibility for one's work and explaining one's decisions to the public.

- Acknowledge mistakes and correct them promptly and prominently.

AN ETHICAL CHALLENGE

Can you buy meals for a lobbyist, a council member or a media-shy subject? The answer is no. Journalists cover the news; they can't influence it, or be influenced by it.

But what if your story is about a starving or homeless family or victims of natural disasters? They're suffering and it won't make much of a dent in your wallet to buy them a few bags of groceries or a night in a hotel room.

What choice do you make? How do you defend that decision? Could you do so in a story?

#21: The Internet Can't Knock On Doors

Many young journalists feel more comfortable sitting at their computers and searching for sources, story ideas and information on the World Wide Web than reporting in the field. On one level it's understandable. Today's students and young journalists are digital natives who are at ease at the computer screen and on their smartphones.

COVID CANCELS FACE-TO-FACE

When the Covid epidemic struck in 2020, the danger of infection kept journalists home. Older journalists struggled with Zoom calls and other technology, while their younger colleagues adapted easily to remote reporting.

In 2021, Jose A. Del Real, a Washington Post reporter in his 30s, had no choice when he reported a story about a family divided by their mother's embrace of conspiracy theories. With travel and in-person reporting hindered by the pandemic, he had to rely on phone calls, emails and texts.

For background, he scoured the internet to find sources who would discuss their interpersonal experiences with political information and conspiracy theories.

"With some keyword magic," he told me in an interview published on Nieman Storyboard, "you can find folks on various social media platforms who have posted about their experiences."

Now that vaccines are available, Del Real is back on the road talking to people in person.

And that's how it should be.

KNOCK, KNOCK

I love the internet, but it's no substitute for coming face-to-face with a human being where they can look you in the eye and decide whether to open up. That's the way you get great quotes and compelling details.

"Basic reporting is not about looking things up on the internet,"' says Carl Bernstein, who, with his reporting partner Bob Woodward at The Washington Post, helped drive President Richard M. Nixon from The White House in 1974 after uncovering his entanglement in the Watergate scandal.

Conscious that many of their sources wouldn't talk at the office, they often showed up at their sources' homes at night to seek information. Many doors were slammed in their faces, but they persisted.

Eventually, a bookkeeper for the Committee to Re-Elect the President agreed to talk and provided damning evidence, the pair recalled in their book "All the President's Men."

"What we need to be doing now is knocking on doors, getting out into the communities we cover, persistence, perpetual engagement with the story, not taking no for answers," Bernstein said in a January 2022 New York Times Book Review podcast.

Be honest: Are you spending too much time on the net instead of out in the community or the area covered by your beat? If you're not on deadline, get out of the office right now. Knock on a door.

I once wrote a story about a man who died of lung cancer after a lifetime of smoking and asked his widow for an interview. I went to her house. I always ask for a tour. She showed me her bedroom. I looked for details, but could only see a small picture of her husband wedged in a mirror. Suddenly, she said, "At night, I sprinkle his aftershave on my pillow. Just to feel close to him." I had the ending for my story.

You can't get that on the internet.

#22: Nasal Congestion

A nose for news. In journalism, the phrase means the ability to sniff out the newsworthy from the trivial. Investigative reporters have one. Give them a whiff of corruption and they'll dig in like a pig rooting for truffles. Narrative writers uncover conflict and discover compelling characters.

Write with the senses, editors and writing teachers demand. The best writers do that, providing readers with vivid images and resonant sounds.

But hunt for a smell in news stories and most days you'll come up empty.

"Smell," wrote the blind and deaf writer Helen Keller, "is a potent wizard that transports you across thousands of miles and all the years you have lived."

Pick a smell and it will take you back to times past, remembered places. I need only catch a whiff of patchouli oil and it's the 1960s again.

"Smells detonate softly in our memory like poignant land mines, hidden under the weedy mass of many years and experiences,"

Diane Ackerman writes in "A Natural History of the Senses." "Hit a tripwire of smell, and memories explode all at once. A complex vision leaps out of the undergrowth."

All of us have a lengthy catalog of smells that make us remember and feel. So why are we so reluctant to employ them in our writing?

Ackerman makes the case that the problem is in our head, in the connections that link our sense of smell with the parts of the brain where language forms. She calls smell "the mute sense, the one without words."

Richard Price, the novelist ("Clockers") and screenwriter ("The Color of Money"), writes powerfully with his nose.

His novels reek, in the very best sense of the word. His olfactory prose offers a master class for journalists intent on bringing this vital sense into their own stories.

THE MADELEINE EFFECT

For French novelist Marcel Proust, taste was the bridge between present and past, captured in a legendary scene in his classic novel, "Remembrance of Things Past." Dipping a madeleine, a small shell-shaped pastry, into a cup of lime-flower tea, enables the narrator to recreate in his mind intense memories from his childhood.

In the gritty world of Price's urban New Jersey wasteland, the smell of cafeteria food is an equally powerful time transporter. The italicized passages are from Price's novel "Samaritan."

"Straightening up, he was struck with a humid waft of boiled hot dogs and some kind of furry bean-based soup that threw him right back into tenth grade."

SENSE AS PLACE

"A greasy aroma drifted down from the third-floor food court— spare ribs and Cinnabons..."

SMELL AS CHARACTER

"Danielle then embraced Ray. She was sporting some kind of vanilla-musk body spray, the scent so dense that it made him dizzy."

SMELL AS MOOD

"It was cold, the city-borne breeze damp and acrid, still damp with dread after all this time."

LEARNING TO SMELL

1. Breathe in

"Each day," Ackerman writes, "we breathe about 23,040 times and move around 438 cubic feet of air. It takes us about five seconds to breathe—two seconds to inhale and three seconds to exhale—and, in that time, molecules of odor flood through our systems."

Our antiseptic age seems designed to rob us of smells or confuse our nose with synthetic concoctions that mask noxious chemicals with the aromas of the orchard.

Cultivate your sense of smell by using it as much as you can.

2. Name that smell

We can detect over 10,000 odors, Ackerman says.

I've asked writers and editors to develop a catalog of smells. Here's a sampling:

- New wood
- Lilacs
- Horse manure
- Dried seaweed
- After summer rain
- Coffee with cream
- Freshly mown grass

3. Describe the smell

Modifiers can heighten a smell's impact. Price regularly uses them in his olfactory details. (Words are in bold for emphasis.)

*"The air smelled of sea funk and overturned earth; the only thing Ray loved about living in Little Venice, the **raw and heady** scent made him think of new beginnings, of second and third chances to get things right."*

4. Find the source

Don't just inhale the world. Identify and describe the smell and the memory or feeling it evokes. "Apartment 27," wrote Anne Hull in the St. Petersburg Times, "smelled like years of sweat and Lemon Pledge and perfect bacon."

#23: Shunning Private Records

Savvy journalists know the value of public records—police reports, courthouse files, meeting transcripts, and other documents generated—and often concealed—by government agencies. (See #31 Letting Your FOIA Garden Go to Seed.)

They furnish authority, libel protection and the occasional smoking gun that makes for powerful journalism and significant reforms.

But there's another, less obvious record type that writers can use to add unforgettable ingredients to their stories.

These are private records, the documentation that people create and keep about their own lives or others', the kind buried in a box in the attic, hanging on the refrigerator door or placed inside a photo album or yearbook.

"People record their lives in all sorts of ways," says Louise Kiernan, a journalism professor at Northwestern University who took advantage of these records when she was a Pulitzer Prize–winning reporter at the Chicago Tribune. "Often what they write or is written about them is more true than what they tell you."

Private records can bring a new level of intimacy and depth to your stories, shedding light on a person's character or a time in history. By simply asking sources to hunt in their attics and basements and memory boxes, journalists can locate records that reveal a character's inner life and history.

Among them: baby books, high school and college yearbooks, playbills for student productions, diaries, journals, letters, photos and videos.

In October 2018, a team of ProPublica Illinois journalists used an unusual private record in an investigative narrative that exposed the human impact of a flawed clinical drug trial at the University of Illinois at Chicago on children with bipolar disorder. They obtained an online journal kept by a mother who recorded the disastrous side effects experienced by her 10-year-old son, who was enrolled in the study. With her permission, the team split the story between their findings and the emotional evidence of a family's torment.

I used public and private records for an essay about my father, who died when I was 10 years old, particularly the impact of his father's involvement in a government corruption scandal in 1932. They included the campus newspaper where he excelled in sports, but also his report card, which showed a precipitous drop when his father's wrongdoing was exposed.

"There may have been other reasons," I wrote, "but I can't help but notice that his poor performance in school dovetailed with the period that legions of New York City newspapers were painting his father as a Tammany Hall grafter."

TIPS

- **Think about private records in your own life.** If someone were to write a story about you, what might they learn from your yearbook, the letters or cards you've kept, your journal entries, photo albums, videotapes?

- **Ask sources for private records.** Investigative reporters know to always ask for public records. Ask for private records as well. Be alert to the possibility that private records might exist.
- **Make private records part of your storytelling.** A Chicago Tribune reporter mined student evaluations to profile a dying professor. In a story about postpartum depression, Kiernan used excerpts from the journal of a woman who had committed suicide.
- **Respect people's privacy.** Ethical journalists will make certain subjects know how their private records will be used. Be wary of invading someone's privacy, which could lead to a lawsuit.

#24: Keeping The Scaffolding

One summer between college semesters, I spent a scary week standing on wooden scaffolding to paint a triple-decker tenement house. I was relieved when the workday ended, and I could climb down from my perch to solid ground. When the job was done, we dismantled the scaffolding, packed the poles and platforms into our truck, and drove away, leaving a freshly painted house.

In journalism, words are the scaffolding you use to construct your stories. The difference between the folks in hard hats and those of us who bang on computer keys is that they dismantle their scaffolding while we often leave ours standing.

How many times have you read—or written—a story that began with the phrase, "This is a story about..."?

It could be property taxes or vaccines or love. In a book review, it's appropriate. In a news story, it's a weak opening and a flabby way to convey a theme.

If you believe your story is about corruption, show it. What is the best example you have—the building inspector who lives in a waterfront mansion paid for with bribes from developers? Lead with that.

LIKELY SCAFFOLDING SUSPECTS

1. Questions

Here are three paragraphs in a story I wrote in The Providence Journal about a rooftop drama when a police officer talked an ex-cop out of killing himself:

The two men talked for nearly two hours as the sun began to fade.

What did they talk about?

"You know, little things, even the way he shined his shoes," Lt. Lawton said. "Anything to keep his mind off jumping or shooting himself."

Cut the extraneous question, paraphrase and end with a memorable quote.

They talked of little things, even the way he shined his shoes. "Anything," Lt. Lawton said, "to keep his mind off jumping or shooting himself."

Shorter and more dramatic. Readers can furnish their own scaffolding. Give them more credit.

2. Transitions

In the 1970s, The Wall Street Journal influenced a generation of news writers with a stable of transitions—indeed, to be sure, what's more, moreover. They sound authoritative. In most cases, they're a waste of the reader's time.

3. Asides

In this chapter's first draft, I used phrases such as "of course," and "that is" to bridge my thoughts. Unnecessarily.

Scaffolding is an essential part of the writing process. But as my former editor Julie Moos said, "Just because it's part of your writing process doesn't mean it should be part of my reading process." Before you submit your story, take it down.

#25: Data Denial

Mention the word *data* and many journalists look like a deer caught in the headlights. We're word people, we say. Data is for geeks.

That attitude denies your audience information in computer databases that reveal hidden secrets and compelling stories. It can cheat you of the chance to do the most exciting and important work in your career.

"Data journalism matters because we live, increasingly, in a data-driven world," Casey Frechette, who teaches and researches data journalism at the University of South Florida's St. Petersburg campus, told me. "The digitization of society means the emergence of limitless troves of information about how businesses operate; how citizens lead their lives; how governments run. In this sea of data, it's easy to find ourselves adrift. Data journalists help us make sense of it all."

STEP INTO DATA JOURNALISM

1.**Acquire**. The Washington Post used newly released tract-level census data for an interactive database that shows, by typing in your address, how the racial makeup of your neighborhood has changed since 1990.

2.**Query**. The data journalist probes the stockpile of information, looking for story ideas in spreadsheets or to confirm key facts from traditional sources, like an interview with a public official.

3.**Analyze**. Using basic math and at times advanced statistics, data journalists find averages, establish ratios and crunch percentages. Sophisticated calculations can establish correlations between two variables, such as tenant evictions and rising rents.

4.**Visualize**. "It's vital," Frechette says, "to enable people to understand what data means. That's where visualization comes in, turning statistics into interactive maps and visual worlds."

Wall Street Journal reporters Joel Eastwood and Erik Hinton achieved that with an algorithm to compile lyrics from the Broadway musical hit "Hamilton" that enabled them to show how creator Lin-Manuel Miranda tapped rap and hip-hop's imperfect, internal rhymes to make musical history. It's very cool!

HUMANIZING DATA

Behind every statistic is a human being. Journalists who don't highlight people in their stories will fail to connect their findings with their audiences.

Numbers numb, according to psychologist Paul Slovic, who co-authored the 2015 study "The More Who Die, the Less We Care." It concluded that "as numbers get larger and larger, we become insensitive; numbers fail to trigger the emotion or feeling necessary to motivate action."

About 700 women die in America every year from pregnancy or delivery complications, according to the U.S. Centers for Disease Control and Prevention, making us the nation with the highest level of maternal mortality in the developed world.

But how to illustrate the problem when most of these deaths are kept hidden by authorities?

ProPublica and NPR reporters overcame that obstacle by creating their own dataset of victims by scouring public posts on Twitter and Facebook and the crowdfunding sites GoFundMe and YouCaring, asking for audience input and using obituaries and public records to verify the women's basic information. Working with student journalists from New York University, they reached out to family members.

"Lost Mothers," the series they produced, presents a photo gallery of 134 women who died giving birth in 2016; 16 of them are feature obituaries. It's a riveting example of how data journalists succeed by putting a human face on the numbers their computers churn out.

#26: Being A Fixer

Two types of editors occupy newsrooms: fixers and coaches.

Fixers, as the name implies, see themselves as repairmen and women. Their job is to take a reporter's story and, without consultation, fix the broken parts.

Lead too wordy? Change it. Paragraph too long? Cut it in half. Mangled prose? Rewrite it.

It all sounds very efficient, unless you're on the receiving end.

Instead, you get the morning paper or open your news site and find that your story has been turned into something you don't recognize. Worse, whoever was responsible for changing it has introduced errors.

Journalists hate fixers, for obvious reasons. But often they are powerless to push back because of their place in the newsroom pecking order.

Editors who coach, by contrast, work side-by-side with reporters to improve their stories. If they find a problem, they talk it over without letting their hands touch the copy. Could the lead be shorter? I stumbled over this passage. How could it be changed?

Coaching imagines the editing craft "as an essentially human rather than technical encounter," according to Roy Peter Clark, who, with the late Don Fry, wrote "Coaching Writers: Editors and Reporters Working Together," the first book on the subject.

Questions and constructive conversations give the writer control.

When Marc Lacey was national editor at The New York Times, he was surprised to learn that his most consequential editing was done with "my voice, not my fingers."

"Giving good feedback at the start and precise recommendations on how to make a piece sing is as important, or even more important, than chopping the prose or moving the paragraphs myself," Lacey, now an assistant managing editor, said in an interview published in my book "Writers on Writing: Inside the Lives of 55 Distinguished Writers and Editors."

Sandy Rowe was The Oregonian's top editor when she realized she had one primary responsibility: "to create and sustain the kind of environment in which talented journalists could do their best work."

If you're lucky enough to have an editor like Lacey or Rowe, your chances of success increase exponentially. You will learn something new with every story you produce. A coaching editor can help you embrace journalism—or turn you off it forever.

COACHING AIMS

Coaching is based on the premise that the power to recognize a story's problems as well as the means to fix them lies within the person reporting and writing the story.

It has four aims, according to the late writing coach Donald M. Murray, who spearheaded the movement to replace fixers:

1. To make use of the knowledge and experience of the writer.
2. To give the writer primary responsibility for the story.
3. To provide an environment in which the writer can do the best possible job.
4. To train the writer, so that editing will be unnecessary.

Coaching does not mean journalists don't need editors, however. In fact, the editor's role is essential to the writing process. Even though reporters know all the problems in their stories as well as the solutions, they often are blind to that knowledge and need someone to help them find their way.

That's why, when I am coaching someone, my first question is, "How can I help?"

That's not a cop-out or touchy-feely approach to the challenging work of journalism. Coaching should never be synonymous with coddling. The best editors challenge, communicate, care and collaborate. "I was frankly amazed," Lacey said, "the first time I told a correspondent how to fix a story in a brief phone conversation and shortly thereafter saw it return transformed."

THE VALUE OF COACHING

Coaching represents a good-faith effort to get the very best out of someone for the benefit of an audience and, by extension, our democratic society that gives journalists enormous advantages and, along with them, enormous responsibilities—accuracy, fairness and care.

Coaching requires active participation, rather than sitting back and waiting for others to tell you what to do.

It's valuable as well because it draws on two basic skills you as a journalist already possess: the ability to ask good questions about a story and the ability to listen to the answers.

1. What's the news?
2. What's the story?
3. Why does it matter?
4. What does it say about life, about the world and the times we live in?
5. What works in your story?
6. What needs work?

I usually write down what the writer I'm coaching tells me, or I ask them to freewrite the answers. Often their responses, with some revision, end up in their stories.

Fixers say there's no time to talk. Coaches understand that the investment pays off as journalists learn to coach themselves.

#27: Time Mismanagement

Complete this sentence:

If I managed my time, my stories, and myself better, I would be

_____.

"Less stressed."

"Getting better evaluations."

"Happier with my stories."

"Covering my beat more effectively."

"Happier" (or as one participant at a workshop cried out, "Married!")

There's no right answer, just the articulation of dreams that can be achieved if we use time as an ally.

Time management is one of the most important self-improvement techniques, but one least utilized by journalists.

Large-scale surveys routinely find time management skills are "among the most desired workforce skills, but at the same time among the rarest skills to find," Erich C. Dierdorff, an editor at Personnel Psychology, wrote in Harvard Business Review.

You feel haunted by the clock, harrowed by deadlines, when, in reality, you can seize control of time.

PRACTICAL APPROACHES

1. Build a "mountain with stairs."

Think of your next story as a "mountain with stairs—a set of smaller steps leading to the top," advises Eviatar Zerubavel in "The Clockwork Muse."

Break it down into its components: idea generation, reporting and research, focusing, planning, drafting, and revising. Assign time estimates to each step. Keep track of the actual time you spend.

The tasks that we think will take a long time are often accomplished more quickly, while those that we think are a snap take more time than we thought. Develop a more accurate gauge of your time expenditure.

2. Work in brief daily sessions.

Productive writers don't chain themselves to their keyboards all day long, psychologist Robert Boice reported in his book "How Writers Journey to Comfort and Fluency: A Psychological Adventure."

What many writers do is binge, Boice says. Especially journalists. They procrastinate for hours, building up a steam of guilt and frustration, and that combination ultimately leads to indifference: "I don't care how bad it is, I've only got 45 minutes left."

They write in a fury until deadline or just after, irritating their editors and ensuring that their copy will be hastily edited. They've robbed their audience of a fresh eye that might spot a confusing sentence or important information buried in the story. And when it's all done, they're exhausted, stressed out and ready for a drink.

Instead, write an early "discovery" draft to find out what you already know and need to know. On daily stories, try to work in 15- to 30-minute drafting sessions, taking short breaks, and then edit and revise.

3. Make friends with a clock.

A timepiece is a way to control the process even if you can't control the material. Your cellphone alarm is ideal. Journalists may not be able to control how well they write, but they can write quickly, leaving time for revision. Set your alarm for the kind of drafting and revision sessions described in the section above.

None of us can guarantee that our stories will be brilliant. But we can better control our time. When we do that, we greatly improve our chances of achieving our dreams of success.

#28: Cliché Collision

Have you ever started a story this way:

"It's that time of year again."

"Webster's defines..."

"It was the best of times. It was the worst of times."

Or written this line:

"... is not alone," as in "Chip is not alone. He's one of millions of people worldwide who thinks their ideas are worth blogging about."

Every one of these examples is a cliché, a tired, overused phrase that is the refuge of writers too lazy or weak to come up with something original.

Clichés are flabby. They weaken the power of prose. They can cost you readers who are looking for writing that is fresh.

PAINT-BY-NUMBERS WRITING

In "The Sound on the Page: Great Writers Talk about Style and Voice in Writing," journalism professor Ben Yagoda defines cliché as "the use, either unconscious or in an attempt to write colorfully or alluringly, of hackneyed or worn-out words, phrases, or figures of speech."

- Only time will tell
- Back in the day
- Mother of all

Clichés are an understandable refuge when you're struggling to make meaning out of words, especially on deadline.

When you're drafting a story, the public domain of words and phrases from popular culture automatically pops into the top of your conscious mind. Before you ~~throw in the towel~~ give up and throw your laptop out the window, ~~cut yourself some slack~~, don't be too hard on yourself. In a way, reliance on clichés is not your fault.

"Clichés are prominent features of everyone's first drafts," Yagoda says. "How could they not be? We hear and read them all the time and our brains are filled with them."

But clichés are deadly, and "their first victim," he says, "is thought."

Clichés deaden the mind. They ignore the reader's demand for originality.

In British writer George Orwell's ~~oft-quoted~~ list of writing rules, "avoid clichés" tops the list.

"Never use a metaphor, simile or other figure of speech which you are used to seeing in print," Orwell wrote.

- Off the rack
- Low-hanging fruit
- A blast from the past
- A sea change

A BUILT-IN CLICHÉ DETECTOR

To dodge clichés, ask yourself if you've ever heard a phrase before and where you heard it. Check online dictionaries to make sure you're using it correctly. The Urban Dictionary is especially useful to detect time-worn slang.

Your ears may be the best weapon you have.

Reading your work aloud improves your chance of recognizing and deleting the commonplace words and phrases that deadline writing or first drafts generate.

- From jump street
- Get-go
- Achilles heel

Turn a cliché around. I once read a story about computer sales that used a phrase "win hearts and minds," which came into currency during the Vietnam War. It screamed cliché. I thought about it for a minute and thought it might have worked better as " win the hearts, minds and modems."

Avoid cliches like the plague and you'll be on cloud nine.

#29: Unsticking The Landing

Journalists struggle with the ending of stories and even sentences. But they can maximize their impact if they end them with the most powerful words.

"Put the best stuff at the end of the sentence," says Steve Padilla, who edits Column One, the destination for compelling storytelling at the Los Angeles Times.

The late writing coach Jim Hayes taught Padilla that an editor can improve a sentence by reordering the words, rather than adding or cutting them, a practice that writers despise. (See #26 "Being a Fixer.")

"I've found," Padilla told me, "that if a sentence can end with gusto, that helps story organization, keeps the sentences bouncing and flings the reader into the next sentence."

He offered this example:

First, the original (italics added for emphasis):

BEAR VALLEY SPRINGS, Calif. — On a warm autumn morning in the Tehachapi Mountains, fish and game warden Bill

Dailey found that the disturbing tip was true. Resting under an oak tree was a pile of elk legs.

Dailey also found a garbage bag containing a tan carpet fiber, a big eyeball, brain tissue and a small piece of yellow plastic.

The flaw in the third sentence, Padilla said, is that the most shocking item in the list—the eyeball—gets lost in the middle. "The spotlight focuses instead on the yellow plastic, and that's boring." So he just slid the eyeball from the middle of the sentence to the end, and that changed everything.

Dailey also found a garbage bag containing a tan carpet fiber, a small piece of yellow plastic, brain tissue and a big eyeball.

Bam!

A TOOL OF EMPHASIS

Another way to think about this is a formula that some teachers use: the 2-3-1 tool of emphasis that Roy Peter Clark describes in "Writing Tools: 55 Essential Strategies for Every Writer."

"Put your best stuff near the beginning and at the end, hide weaker stuff in the middle," Clark says.

Padilla concedes that some sentences must ignore this approach and end with workaday attributions, such as "according to court records" and "a police spokeswoman said." "But the words just before those should be powerful, interesting or important."

2-3-1 IN QUOTES

You can also use the formula to good effect in quotations, by splitting a quote in half, and dropping attribution in the middle.

Here's a brief example from a story by Jeffrey Gettleman of The New York Times about two sisters killed as their cars collided as they traveled to meet each other.

"They weren't fancy women," (2) said their sister Billie Walker. (3) "They loved good conversation. And sugar biscuits." (1)

The biggest plus of rearranging words may be morale, Padilla pointed out. The practice maintains the writer's words, but merely reorders them, rather than the dispiriting experience of having an editor overhaul your entire sentence.

This way, journalists who adopt the 2-3-1 formula can experience the writer's equivalent of the joy gymnasts feel when they stick the landing.

#30: Covering Politics Like A Horse Race

Political reporters are like sportswriters. When election season arrives, they're fixated on who's winning or losing. The horse race is on, and they're training their eyes on which candidate is moving into position, by what margin and why.

Dazzled by a flood of polls that inundates the political landscape —more than one new poll each day during the 2016 presidential general election, a study found—journalists take their eyes off the issues of policy that reveal what nominees promise they would do if elected.

AND THEY'RE OFF!

"In the 2016 general election, policy issues accounted for 10 percent of the news coverage—less than a fourth the space given to the horserace," concluded Harvard professor Thomas E. Patterson after an exhaustive study of news coverage during the race between Democrat Hillary Clinton and Republican Donald J. Trump.

This graphic shows the breakdown in the contents of campaign coverage from August until Election Day 2016.

percentage of news reports

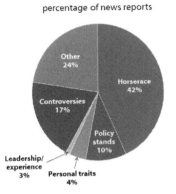

Source: Media Tenor. "Other" refers to staffing issues, logistics and upcoming events. Reprinted with permission.

On the campaign stump, candidates lay out their policies, but "their stands do not receive close attention from journalists," Patterson found.

Delving into policy issues means talking with experts, interest groups and citizens. Writing effectively about policy is hard, as I found out repeatedly during the five years I spent as a Washington correspondent.

Putting a human face on abstract proposals requires time—a precious commodity in the news business—and effort from news teams. Polls, on the other hand, give journalists just what they like: fresh material that's easy to produce.

NOW YOU'VE STEPPED IN IT

Everyone pays the price for horse race coverage. According to Harvard's Shorenstein Center on Media, Politics and Public Policy, decades of academic studies link it to:

1. Distrust of politicians
2. Distrust of news outlets
3. An uninformed electorate

Female political candidates, "who tend to focus on policy issues to build credibility," get shortchanged, the studies found, as do third-party candidates, because they lag behind in the polls.

The advantage goes to "novel and unusual candidates," like Trump, a businessman who never held public office before running for president.

PULLING ON THE REINS

Newsroom standards on which polls to use and how to judge their relative quality have eroded, a 2019 study found. Relying on polling aggregator websites and dubious online surveys causes journalists to overestimate polling's ability to predict election results. On Election Day 2016, The New York Times said, " Hillary Clinton has an 85% chance to win" the presidency.

Young journalists and those who work for news websites don't always see it as their job to interpret polls for the public and think readers should help. "In a lot of ways Twitter is our ombudsman," an online journalist told researcher Benjamin Toff, a University of Minnesota journalism professor.

That's frightening. Crowdsourcing can be an effective way to enhance content. But it comes with a steep cost when it means turning loose dubious polling data online.

You rein in horse race coverage, experts say, by training journalists to better understand polls. Here are questions the Shorenstein Center says you should ask:

1. Who conducted the poll?
2. Who paid for it?
3. How were people chosen to participate?
4. How was the poll conducted?
5. What's the margin of error?
6. Were participants compensated?

7. Who answered questions?
8. How many people responded to the poll?
9. What did pollsters ask?
10. What might have gone wrong with this poll?

What you learn may not make it into your story, but it could influence whether you run the poll or decide to focus on candidates' policies instead. That better serves democracy.

#31: Letting Your FOIA Garden Go To Seed

Sunshine is the best disinfectant.

That's the animating principle behind so-called Sunshine Freedom of Information laws that determine what public agencies on the federal and state levels can keep secret from the public.

Wielded by a determined journalist, they're also a crowbar that can pry out those secrets.

If you aren't taking advantage of the federal Freedom of Information Act statute, informally known as FOIA (pronounced "Foy-yah"), and similar laws, you're depriving your audience of crucial information about the institutions that govern their lives.

"Everyone should know how to file a FOIA request," said Louise Kiernan, former Midwest editor of ProPublica, a nonprofit newsroom that investigates abuses of power by government, businesses and other institutions. The Reporters Committee for Freedom of the Press is an ideal place to learn these skills.

Dave Philipps, a reporter for The Colorado Springs Gazette, used a FOIA request to check out a hunch that the army was discharging soldiers with PTSD and other injuries, in the process giving up their veterans benefits.

"A Gazette investigation based on data obtained through the Freedom of Information Act," Philipps wrote, "shows the annual number of misconduct discharges is up more than 25 percent Army-wide since 2009, mirroring the rise in wounded... All told, more than 76,000 soldiers have been kicked out of the Army since 2006." The series, "Other Than Honorable," won a Pulitzer Prize for national reporting.

FOIA TIPS

1. Be precise

The more complete a request, the better the chances of success, according to a 2017 study of 33,000 FOIA requests published in the Columbia Journalism Review.

Just 17 percent of tweet-sized requests—" throwaways" sent without any serious effort, researchers said—succeeded.

The chance of receiving records jumped when a longer request offered more precise information. FOIA requests to the U.S. Environmental Protection Agency were more successful—64 percent—when they included identification numbers about sites and facilities.

Philipps specifically asked for records on soldiers given Chapter 10 discharges for misconduct. "Around six weeks later, he received a bunch of spreadsheets in the mail," Nieman Lab reported.

"Do as much reporting as possible about the records you are seeking before making the request," Ira Chinoy, a former investigative reporter for The Washington Post, told me. "What state or federal law or regulation spells out what records are to be kept? How are they to be kept, and by whom?" Despite the name of the law, "what you seek are records, not information."

2. Find a human being

Addressing your request to "Madam FOIA Officer" is a surefire fail, the CJR study found. Of 900 such impersonal requests filed, "almost none" received all the records requested.

Find out the name, email and phone number of the agency's FOIA officer. Cultivate a relationship. Ask about the records and how they're kept. Twice in my career, I obtained gigabytes of digital records without having to file a FOIA request because I knew what to ask for.

3. Don't give up

Filing the request may be just the first step on a road filled with obstacles: interminable delays, denials, and exorbitant copy and research costs imposed by recalcitrant bureaucrats. Often records aren't released without the news organization taking the agency to court. It cost the Kansas City Star $43,000 in legal fees to get records about a police officer involved in a fatal shooting.

4. Be patient but persistent

Pepper FOIA officials with frequent calls and emails for updates, and argue against exorbitant fees, advises investigative reporter Katherine Boo, who was awarded a MacArthur Foundation "genius" fellowship for her poverty coverage. Don't let your demands wilt in a bureaucratic thicket. "Tend your FOIAs," Boo said, "like a garden." Nourish them with constant attention until you harvest the information you seek.

#32: Fearing Imitation

In the early 1800s, an English writer named Charles Caleb Colton published a book of aphorisms, including one still popular today: "Imitation is the sincerest of flattery." ("Form," added later, rounds out the way we know it today.)

But for those of us trying to become better writers, imitation is more than flattery; it's a powerful and time-honored way to master the craft. "Numerous writers—Somerset Maugham and Joan Didion come to mind—recall copying long passages verbatim from favorite writers, learning with every line," says Stephen Koch in "The Modern Library's Writer's Workshop."

LEARN FROM THE BEST

Over the years, I've learned important lessons by copying out lines, passages, even entire stories, by writers whose work I admire and would like to emulate.

Typing Wall Street Journal features taught me the anatomy of a "nut graf," journalese for that section of context high up in a story that tells readers what a story is about and why they should read it.

You can discover your own voice by listening to other writers. One of the best ways to listen is by copying out their words.

This practice horrifies some respected writers and teachers; write your own darn stories, they say. But if we were visual artists, would anyone look askance at visiting a museum to try to copy the paintings to see how accomplished artists used color and shadow and contrast?

I'm not talking about plagiarism. Rather, modeling is copying stories to gain a more intimate understanding of the variety of decisions that writers make to organize material, select language and shape sentences.

A WARNING SIGN

Now's a good time for my one caveat about modeling lessons: Always write the writer's byline at the top of the story you're copying in case you get deluded and later confuse someone else's writing with your own.

With the story properly credited, I start typing.

When something strikes me, I'll start to record my observations:

Wow, notice how that long sentence is followed by a short, three-word one, stopping me in my tracks to pay attention. Varying sentence length is a good way to affect pace.

See how Carol McCabe's leads follow a pattern? ("Cold rain spattered on the sand outside the gray house where Worthe Sutherland and his wife Channie P. Sutherland live." "The Bicentennial tourists flowed through Paul Revere's Mall." "Three trailer trucks growled impatiently as a frail black buggy turned onto Route 340.") Subject-Verb-Object. Concrete nouns, vivid active verbs. I've got to do that more.

Every writer, including broadcast and online writers, can profit equally from copying successful stories in their medium.

Pay attention to what the writer is doing and what effect it has on you, the reader. Effective writing is about impact, and writers need to learn how to make one, using all the tools at their disposal.

"Do not fear imitation," says Stephen Koch. "Nobody sensible pursues an imitative style as a long-term goal, but all accomplished writers know that the notion of pure originality is a childish fantasy. Up to a point, imitation is the path to discovery and essential to growth."

In the end, you must use your own words to become the writer you want to be, but I've profited from learning how other writers used theirs. You can too.

#33: Tell Me An Article, Daddy!

Story.

It's a word that echoes in newsrooms every day.

"Great story today."

"Where's that story? You're 30 minutes late!"

"Boss, I need another day/[week/month] to finish that story."

"How the heck did that story get on the front page? (This always refers to another journalist's work.)

And the old standby: "Story at 11."

We call them stories, but most of what appears in print, online and broadcast are articles or reports, says writing teacher Jack Hart.

Here's an example from The Guardian about the February 2022 Russian invasion of Ukraine:

Fierce fighting broke out in Kyiv as Russian forces tried to push their way towards the city centre from multiple directions in the early hours of Saturday, and as the Ukrainian president, Volodomyr

Zelenskiy, bluntly rejected a US offer to evacuate him from the country's capital.

Articles present information about an accident, a public meeting, a speech, a contested presidential election or even a war. They're a convenient way to convey information in a clear, concise, accurate fashion told in a neutral voice.

But please, let's not confuse them with stories.

A story features characters rather than sources and communicates experience through the five senses and a few other elements: place, time and, most all, drama.

It has a beginning that grabs a reader's attention, a middle that keeps the reader engaged and an ending that lingers. Scenes peppered with dialogue and a distinct voice drive the action.

Here's how Mitchell S. Jackson opened "Twelve Seconds and a Life," his Runner's World story about the murder of Ahmaud Arbery, a Black man, by three white men in 2020 as he jogged through their suburban Georgia neighborhood.

Imagine young Ahmaud "Maud" Arbery, a junior varsity scatback turned undersized varsity linebacker on a practice field of the Brunswick High Pirates. The head coach has divided the squad into offense and defense and has his offense running the plays of their next opponent. The coach, as is his habit, has been taunting his defense. "Y'all ain't ready," he says. "You can't stop us," he says. "What y'all gone do?" The next play, Maud, all 5 feet 10 inches and 165 pounds of him, bursts between blockers and—BOOM!— lays a hit that makes the sound of cars crashing, that echoes across the field and into the stands, that just might reach the locker room.

Jackson's story won the 2021 Pulitzer Prize and a National Magazine Award for feature writing.

Journalists must be able to write articles and stories. Each has its own challenges. Articles compress events and focus on newsworthy elements. Stories, also known as narratives, connect us with the universals of the human condition. They matter because they transport us to different worlds that reveal the personal and emotional realities behind the news.

We need stories, nonfiction author Bill Buford wrote in a 1996 essay, because "they are a fundamental unit of knowledge, the foundation of memory, essential to the way we make sense of our lives: the beginning, middle and end of our personal and collective trajectories...because it is impossible to live without them."

Articles have their place, but late at night, your child will never say, "I can't sleep. Tell me an article, Daddy!"

No, they beg to be lulled into slumber by a story.

Instead, in much of news writing, we provide few if any of these.

Instead of settings, we give readers an address.

Instead of characters, we give people stick figures: "Goldilocks, 7, of 5624 Sylvan Way."

Instead of suspense, we give away the ending at the beginning using the inverted pyramid, the form which presents newsworthy elements in descending order and peters out at the end.

The challenge for today's journalists is to use literary techniques to write true stories that, as Joel Rawson, former editor of The Providence Journal, described it, reveal the "joys and costs of being human."

STORYTELLING TIPS

- Newspapers are full of stories waiting to be told. Police briefs, classified ads, obituaries, the last two paragraphs of a city council story; all may hold the promise of a dramatic story. Mine your paper for story ideas.

- Find the extraordinary in the ordinary stuff of life: graduations, reunions, burials, buying a car, putting Mom in a nursing home or the day Dad comes to live with his children.
- Change your point of view. Write the city council story through the eyes of the Asian American who asks for better police protection in his neighborhood.
- Study examples of outstanding narrative nonfiction on these sites: Pulitzer.org, National Magazine Awards, News Leaders Association and Nieman Storyboard.
- Look for ways to drop storytelling features in your daily articles: a description, a scene, a snatch of dialogue.

Bonus Chapter: Help For Luddites

Journalists must juggle assignments, deadlines and research to do their job. The age of fake news, social media and rapidly changing technologies makes their jobs tougher than ever before. A digital toolkit can help you stay organized and ensure that your stories are solidly researched and accurate.

Here are six crucial tools:

Text-to-speech reader. You've proofread your stories, but errors, like gremlins, keep surfacing. This software, installed in System Preferences on PCs and MacBooks, reads back Word and Google documents, emails and text on websites, letting you stop and start with a simple keyboard command. It makes copy cleaner, smoother and less prone to gaffes.

Task managers. From Todoist to Trello, journalists have a wide range of free and paid software to keep track of appointments, events and other items. I'm partial to Things, which syncs with my calendars and lets me know day by day what I'm supposed to take care of. You create areas such as Story Ideas, with projects nestled beneath. The todo function is the heart of Things, which enables you to slot them in the appropriate buckets. It's paid software.

Otter.ai. If you're sick of transcribing your interviews, Otter will do it for you. Powered by artificial intelligence, it creates a searchable, hyperlinked transcript in minutes. The mobile version works simultaneously with your smartphone's call recorder to transcribe calls in real time. It's not perfect, but you can have it read back the recording and edit it. Best of all, the first 600 minutes a month are free.

Password Managers. LastPass, Dashlane and 1Pass are the "most impactful" online tools from the last few years, according to Ren LaForme, managing editor of Poynter Online. "No more using the same password across every website. No more forgetting passwords and having to reset them. No more little pieces of paper pinned to the wall near your desk. Just sweet, sweet secure and automatically generated passwords that are available at the click of a button," he wrote in 2018. Some are free, others have a monthly fee. Most major browsers also now offer their own built-in password-management tools and sync across devices.

Google Search. Twenty-five years after its launch, Google remains the portal to the internet. It dominates the search engine market, connecting millions to content every hour. For journalists, it's an indispensable research tool, but one that's often underutilized. Advanced search options—booleans, quoted searches, site and filetype-specific searches, date-range searches and more—can unlock great power, connecting reporters to previously undiscovered public documents and information snippets that can transform their stories.

Google Translate. After Russian troops invaded Ukraine in February 2022, the country's top TV companies issued a statement declaring that they had suspended all commercial breaks to continuously broadcast news updates. In New York, CNN media reporter Oliver Darcy used Google Translate to report their vow "to defend the information space, to cover events as widely as possible, to debunk fakes and to convey to Ukrainians the most important messages as quickly as possible."

Machine learning powers this constantly fine-tuned online translator. In small newsrooms, a shortage of reporters who speak other languages limits outreach to foreign-language communities. The 24-newspaper chain Pamplin Media Group is exploring the use of Google Translate for some stories to reach residents who don't read English, Nieman Lab reported. It's not perfect (some translations are laughable), conceded executive editor John Schrag, but, he added, the Latinx communities approached with the content appreciated the effort. Experts warn, however, against the pitfalls of botched translations and suggest using other sites and crowdsourcing translators to ensure accuracy.

Acknowledgments

To acknowledge all the people who shaped me as a journalist, teacher and writing coach would take too many pages to list, but I'll try.

Melissa Wilson of Networlding Publishing generously gave me the opportunity to join the "33 Ways" community and has been a constant source of rich inspiration and outstanding editorial and marketing support. From start to finish, Becky Blanton has been a fount of ideas, feedback and friendship. Casey Frechette, my former e-learning collaborator at The Poynter Institute, who now directs the journalism program at the University of South Florida St. Petersburg, was never too busy to open a Google Doc and give me invaluable feedback and indefatigable copyediting. His pedagogical and research skills helped buttress several chapters. Jacqui Banaszynski, editor of Nieman Storyboard, a Harvard-sponsored global website that celebrates narrative nonfiction, has afforded me numerous opportunities to interview leading journalists to go behind-the-stories of remarkable narrative journalism.

I'd like to thank the journalists, writers and editors who allowed me to conduct the interviews with them that became my latest books "Writers on Writing: Inside the Lives of 55 Distinguished Writers and Editors" and "Writers on Writing: The Journal." Their insights infuse this book. I'm grateful for the stories and real-world examples other journalists provided.

I have had the great fortune to work with or become friends with a number of brilliant editors and publishers, past and present, who shared their experiences or helped me become a better journalist and coach. They include Paul Tash (Tampa Bay Times), Peter Bhatia (Detroit Free Press), Sandy Rowe (The Oregonian), Sewell Chan (The Texas Tribune), Bob Mong (Dallas Morning News), Joel Rawson (The Providence Journal), Steve Padilla (Los Angeles Times), Alan Rosenberg (The Providence Journal), Jan Winburn (CNN), Bill Marimow (The Philadelphia Inquirer and NPR) and Mark Silverman (The Detroit News).

Melvin Mencher, my professor at the Columbia University Graduate School of Journalism, taught me the role of a journalist in a democracy, and at 95, continues to instruct me. The late Donald M. Murray of the University of New Hampshire, who was my mentor and best friend, taught me everything I know about teaching writing and coaching writers. I miss him every day.

Facebook and LinkedIn friends provided excellent examples of screw-ups. Thanks to Gerry Goldstein, M. Charles Bakst, James Asher, Mark Johnson, Alex Groff, Annette Ayre, Brad Snyder, Carol Fahy, Elizabeth Carr and Jack Zibluk.

Sree Sreenivasan of Arizona State University's Walter Cronkite School of Journalism and Mass Communication has been my guide to social media since we met in 1994. Stephen Buckley let me audition two of these chapters with his reporting class at Duke University. I benefited greatly from many conversations with Elaine Monaghan, a former Reuters foreign correspondent who teaches journalism at The Media School at Indiana University. Sue Horner's guidance on the effective use of numbers was very helpful. I am very grateful to Tom Rosenstiel and Ira Chinoy for providing exceptional insights, respectively, on the challenges of enuring accuracy and the Freedom of Information Act.

A special thanks to Anne Janzer whose book "33 Ways Not To Screw Up Your Business Emails" served as a vital model for mine and who very generously agreed to be an alpha reader of my manuscript and share her astute publishing and marketing knowledge. I owe enormous gratitude to Mark Rhynsburger, who was the final proofreading and copyediting eyes on my book, and whose microscopic attention to detail is an author's dream.

For 15 years, The Poynter Institute was my home. The work I did there, with support from friends and colleagues like Bob Haiman, Karen Dunlap, the late Jim Naughton, Keith Woods, Stephen Buckley, Roy Peter Clark, Wendy Wallace, Vicki Krueger, Julie Moos, Bill Mitchell, Kelly McBride, Al Tompkins, Butch Ward, Andrew Barnes, Scott Libin, Kenny Irby, Howard Finberg, Jill Geisler, Rick Edmonds, Omar Schwanzer, Ren LaForme, Nancy Emineth, Mallary Tenore, Jeff Saffan, Lanette Miller, Bobbi Alsina, David Shedden, Billie Keirstead, and the late Paul Pohlman, Christine Martin and Tommy Carden provided an incubator to learn my new craft as a teacher and coach. Bob Steele, who led the Institute's ethics group, was good enough to review my ethics chapter and made valuable suggestions. Aly Colón, who taught diversity, pitched in as well. The publishers of my two journalism textbooks, Harcourt College Publishers and Oxford University Press, provided expansive space to share the lessons I'd learned about journalism with students and teachers.

My family remains the bulwark of my writing life. Katharine Fair always provides superb copyediting and unstinting support. For nearly five decades, she has been my most astute reader. Loving thanks to her, our three daughters, Caitlin, Lianna, Michaela, my son-in-law, Klein Grimes, and especially my grandchildren, Henry, Theodore and Eleanor Grimes, who remained patient when "Chipper" was too busy writing to read or play.

The worst part of writing acknowledgments is the certainty that you are leaving someone out. In that spirit, a nod goes to Leo, my one-eyed miniature schnauzer, who rousted me from my desk for five or six walks a day. My apologies and thanks to all the rest of you who made this book possible. Your unsung contributions represent Ernest Hemingway's theory of omission (see #8 Iceberg Right Ahead!) at work.

Before You Go

Trying to cover all the bases of a complex profession like journalism in 33 short chapters is a daunting task. Let me know what you think about the book, whether it helped you do your job as a journalist or teacher, encouraged you to become a journalist or raised a question in your mind. You can reach me at chipscan@gmail.com.

I'd appreciate it if you'd leave an honest review if and wherever you buy it. Sharing your views will, I hope, reach others interested in journalism.

Every two weeks, I publish a free writing advice newsletter, Chip's Writing Lessons. I invite you to join me as I interview leading writers and editors, provide craft lessons like the kind found within these covers, and offer recommendations for reading and listening and a tip of the week. You can subscribe at chipscanlan.-substack.com. Paid subscribers receive a package of extras—additional interviews, behind-the-story looks at journalistic excellence and more.

Finally, at a time when global conflicts seem to erupt every day, please consider donating to the Committee to Protect Journalists, cpj.org, a nonprofit that works to promote press freedom worldwide. One of its important—and tragic—roles is to tally the number of journalists intimidated, imprisoned or killed since 1992—as of March 2022, 1,440 deaths and rising every day. Defending the people's right to know, whether it's in a local community or on a battlefield, has never been more critical.

More 33 Ways

Want more great read-and-learn today and implement tomorrow 33 Ways books? Check these out:

Other Books in the 33 Ways Series

33 Ways Not to Screw Up Your Business Emails

33 Ways Not to Screw Up Consulting

33 Ways Not to Screw Up Creative Entrepreneurship

33 Ways Not to Screw Up Cyber Security

33 Ways Not to Screw Up Your Financial Life

33 Ways Not to Screw Up Your Journalism

33 Ways Not to Screw Up Hiring Great Talent

Link to these on: 33WaysSeries.com

About the Author

Christopher "Chip" Scanlan started out in news delivering his hometown paper, The Greenwich (Connecticut) Time. For two decades, he worked as an award-winning beat and general assignment reporter, feature writer, investigative reporter and Washington correspondent in newsrooms big and small.

Since 1994, he has coached writers and editors around the globe. He is the former director of writing programs and the National Writer's Workshops at The Poynter Institute, one of the world's top schools for professional journalists.

Chip has authored or edited a dozen books, including anthologies of prize-winning journalism, a novel, "The Holly Wreath Man" (co-written with Katharine Fair), two journalism textbooks, and most recently "Writers on Writing: Inside the Lives of 55 Distinguished Writers and Editors" and "Writers on Writing: The Journal."

His nonfiction and fiction have appeared in The New York Times, The Washington Post Sunday Magazine, Salon.com, NPR, Redbook, The American Scholar, Elysian Fields, River Teeth, and Sunday Short Reads, among numerous other publications. Two of his essays were selected as "Notables" in the annual "Best American Essays" series. He is a regular contributor to Nieman Storyboard. His writing advice newsletter, Chip's Writing Lessons, can be found at chipscanlan.substack.com. He writes and coaches from his home in St. Petersburg, Florida, and is available at chipscan@gmail.com.

Made in the USA
Columbia, SC
24 July 2023

20823432R00076

33 WAYS NOT TO SCREW UP YOUR JOURNALISM

33 Ways Series

CHIP SCANLAN

net worlding PUBLISHING

33 Ways Not To Screw Up Your Journalism

Chip Scanlan

Networlding Publishing

For more information or for bulk sales, contact chipscan@gmail.com

Paperback ISBN: 978-1-955750-30-1
Ebook ISBN: 978-1-955750-31-8